Conversations
with
Berenson

Conversations
with
Berenson

Umberto Morra

Translated from the Italian
by Florence Hammond

HOUGHTON MIFFLIN COMPANY BOSTON
The Riverside Press Cambridge
1965

GRATEFUL acknowledgment is made to
Mr. Diarmuid Russell and Mr. Girolamo Vitelli
for their invaluable help in clarifying
certain details of the translation.

F. H.

Foreword

FROM 1931 to 1940 it happened that I took notes, sporadically, on the conversations which I had with Berenson, or on talks of his which I heard while I was a guest in his house. My welcome into the household had begun some years before, in the summer of 1925, at the time of the imprisonment of his very great friend, Gaetano Salvemini. I had made my way up to I Tatti, Berenson's villa on the hills of Settignano, with a sort of friendly "mission" which could not be entrusted to the mail or to anybody in the least unreliable. This granted me easy access and meant that I was immediately received into the not very large company of his friends without having to stand in line or pass an examination, and thus began one of the truly outstanding privileges I experienced during my younger years.

All those who have ever frequented Bernard Berenson know what his conversation meant — its rapid transitions from whiplash epigrams to tones of thoughtful wisdom, and its continuous references drawn from a richness of cultural,

worldly and artistic experience, a knowledge of the past and
of the present, of men and of nations, which was shared with
very few people in his own time and which was perhaps by
no one so liberally incorporated into even the most casual
interchanges between friends, acquaintances, or perfect
strangers. Many times people would present themselves at I
Tatti, motivated by little more than curiosity, and no matter
how little affinity he might have felt with them, or how little
they might have inspired him in any way, Berenson was generous with his time and with his attention, listening to them
and letting himself be drawn into long, subtle, and unfore-
seeable discourses. The truth was that Berenson enjoyed
conversation; for him it was equally a "game for the spirit"
and a total concern, something both beguiling and altogether
serious, and it therefore mattered to him that, at least in
embryo, the same delight, the same seriousness be brought
to bear by the person talking with him — by whoever was
furnishing him with the pretext, or putting him in the mood,
for "thinking aloud." Berenson did not care whether or not
these scattered crumbs of his knowledge and of his feelings
were thrown out and lost, but whoever heard him was conscious of its often being far more than a matter of crumbs,
and that there was the immediate danger that an entire train
of thought, pursued insistently by him sometimes for several days at a time, with ideas which were enunciated and
"thought out" in conversation before being consigned to
paper, might remain forever in that state. For this reason
I resolved one day to transcribe as much as possible of what
struck me in his talks the moment I left his company — to

set down on paper some of those things he said which were so pungent and burning (and these were the easiest to bear in mind, accurately, word for word) — to go over again, painstakingly, all the ground which his sinuous thought had covered in one of those talks during which at times it had been difficult to see just where his subtlety was directed. The subjects he touched on were of all kinds: from politics to the arts, from anecdotes to almost philosophical pronouncements. I make no pretense of being able to render the liveliness and the richness of his reasoning, the graphic quality of his examples; but I have tried to remain faithful to his words, or at least to the sense and progression of his talk, and not to falsify his opinions. This task was less difficult for me when it was a question of literary or historical themes, and more taxing to my lesser experience if the discourse fell upon matters pertaining to art. But not even in the latter case did I want to refrain from making a record, even though that was a field wherein the talk would often repeat theories or opinions which were already published, or anticipate something which Berenson might go on to set down more fully in an article or a book. It always seemed to me that his own words — if they were strictly interpreted and hardly "touched up" at all — would still be able to add something to his hypothetical written work — a renewed immediacy and a fresher dimension.

Careful revision of these notes of mine — particularly the parts which treat of the visual arts — was conducted by Luisa Nicolson Vertova, a person of long familiarity with Berenson's work and thought, both of which benefited in his last years from her competent help. Words and phrases are sometimes quoted in languages other than Italian, when it seemed to me that the timbre of his personality would be better rendered in the language in which they had been spoken — English or French. But Berenson had a prodigious command of Italian; it was not always pedantically correct, but was full of variety, surprising variety, in vocabulary, enriched by his habitual acquaintance with our good writers but also redolent of colloquialisms and sayings which were unmistakably his own.

A tape recorder would have been better than a volunteer amanuensis, but in those years they were not yet available, and Berenson would never have been able to adapt himself to the presence of a mechanical instrument. The simple supposition of why it was there would have paralyzed his talk, which, it is superfluous to add, he had no idea would be transcribed. I was certain that only by keeping quiet as to my intentions would I leave it free to flow forth naturally and unpremeditatedly.

UMBERTO MORRA

Conversations

with

Berenson

January 31–February 1, 1931
TODAY for the first time the Queen Mother of Albania is mentioned in the newspapers. This reminds me of a delightful story about Camondo.

Camondo, of the Camondo collection, was a young Jewish banker of Turkish origin who was of great service to Napoleon III. The emperor wanted to recompense him, and had sounded him out to see whether a title might satisfy him. "A title? But Sire, that would be ridiculous: everyone here knows that I am a banker, there is no use to me in leaving my walk of life, and furthermore I take care of my own interests and withhold whatever means are necessary for my work, so I have no need of reward." His services continued, of all kinds, and the emperor felt his indebtedness mounting; he did not know what to do, but to put his own mind at ease he once again suggested the title. "Sire, if truly you want to give me a recompense of this sort, I cannot ask it for myself, but there is my poor great-grandfather who lives in Constan-

tinople, and he is old, and they have persecuted and
scorned him all his life; I do not ask this for myself, but for
him, poor man, so that he may satisfy his vanity before going to his eternal rest." And thus Camondo the younger obtained a title plus the benefits of a title, that is, the ancestors
and almost the four quarterings of nobility.

With the snow high on the mountains all around and va-
pors of fog in the valleys going down to the Arno, this could
be a Japanese landscape . . . However, even in our imagi-
nations we do not realize how a Japanese landscape really
looks: our fancy passes over the most obvious elements of
that landscape, its immediate foreground. For example, the
ordering and distribution of the fields: Anglo-Americans
are acquainted with a certain arrangement of fields in
landscapes which occurs throughout England and America,
so that even coming onto the Continent is quite a surprise.
But in Japan there are rice paddies, and here there are
fields of wheat; all we have to do is to think what rice paddies are like in Lombardy and it is already a rather alarming spectacle. The Japanese will have adorned and "done"
his landscape in a way which we do not suspect, we who persist in "doing" a landscape each time we look at it — each
time with greater penetration, bringing to it our accumulated
memories and whatever artistic experience we have acquired.
What is "nature" in the landscape? Very little of what one
sees, and discernment and application are necessary in dis-
tinguishing it from the (naturalistic) work of man.

In the lectures K.S. is preparing for Cambridge she speaks of the mouth as a sexual chimney; madmen, she says, who no longer want to open their mouths to eat, will, in explaining their madness, declare nine times out of ten that they are not eating because they know that the food is poisoned; however, she immediately connects this refusal of food with some infantile reaction originating at the time of breast feeding: premature separation from the breast, a repressed desire to suckle. Why, why should I accept, should I believe this explanation, when that other (the fear of poisoning) is logical, and is founded on any number of historical and immediate facts? Even if some cure based on the latter hypothesis should succeed, the fact does not signify much: people can be cured by any theory whatever, so long as they are disposed to believe in the cure, or if there be implicit in it some almost suggestive, miraculous force. Cures do not prove anything. One would have to be able to "repeat" the whole experiment, that is, besides curing, to remove the initial "repressions" and to actually cause the madness by "repressing."

A critic's finest hour comes in his twenties, when he seems bound and able to rebuild everything he comes across. — What about Ojetti? — Ojetti[1] is a literary man. — Sainte-Beuve? — Sainte-Beuve is an essayist, a psychological writer, and above all a historian, who completely and perfectly reconstructs the atmosphere in which he, the author, moves.

[1] Ugo Ojetti, critic and connoisseur.

— Strachey? — Strachey is a historian pure and simple, when he does something good.

Just what will it amount to, the Irish government's attempt to revive a language which for at least a hundred years has been losing currency to the point of annihilation? Can there ever be a new Gaelic literature, or will it just represent an effort on the part of erudite folklorists to revive it from books, or from their own booklike minds? There have already been similar examples; no matter how perfect, a literature born in this fashion is a literature which lacks lymph and air; it is refuted by its own translations which, if at all adequate, are better than the originals. Poliziano's Latin poems, or Sannazzaro, translated by the poets of the Pléiade and above all by Spenser, gain in translation: Spenser's age was one of the richest moments of the English language, full of juices and exuberance, whereas Latin on the other hand was a thoroughly dead language, and any attempt to try to revive it a vain endeavor. At first, with medieval hymns, Latin was still a live thing — already decadent, but alive, attached to the soil, capable of development. With Sanskrit the same thing occurred. The *Ghitago-winda* is a very late poem, and one can hardly read it in the original, whereas the translations are perfect.

The father of T. died at the age of ninety and lost everyone beforehand. One should prepare oneself with young friends for one's old age, and transfer the enjoyment of life from oneself to them.

February 2, 1931

The various religious orders in the Orient are rich in people of the highest quality: the Assumptionists at Constantinople (much better than their colleagues in France), the French Jesuits in Beirut, the Italian Franciscans in Palestine, and even the Spanish Franciscans, who are beautiful types, albeit poorer intellectually. The most extraordinary of those I have met is Father B. who was an officer during the war and remained a businessman afterward. He has intellectual clarity and is extraordinarily cultivated, but is nevertheless sincerely devout, which is difficult for a Catholic because the Catholics are used to, are driven to, reasoning, whereas for Protestants it is easier to make a comfortable mishmash of faith and reason. The scholarly works and journals which these orders publish are done with utmost care and are scientifically perfect; the Church does not forbid, but in fact urges factual research, and is never alarmed by the conclusions so long as they appear as "historical" and do not become a springboard for plunging into dogma.

A pity that Catholicism, in America, is marked with the Irish stamp, that is to say composed almost entirely (in its hierarchy and guiding spirit) of Irishmen. If native German Catholics had more force there it would be a good thing. America needs Catholicism, needs to be taught the discernment of spiritual dimensions, a respect for the greatnesses and the difficulties of life. Catholicism carries with it the

tragic sense of human relationships and ennobles physiological necessities by attributing to them the sense of sin. —
Isn't this only the Jansenist aspect? — But Jansenism (not in
the dogmatic, but in the moral sense) is latent in Catholicism, manifesting itself when men's spirits are sufficiently
lofty, and attentive, and aware: it exists among the German,
French and Belgian Catholics, also among the Italians (in
centers such as Milan and Florence) and the Irish in Ireland; when the Irish go to America they lose their nobility
and become the most American of all. The American semi-
narists in Rome nearly die laughing at the inefficiency, the
impracticality, the non-progressiveness of the Church; they
would like to run it like the Ford Motor Company. Catholicism in America — it should be a cure for that universal
swampiness, or for whatever it is that makes American life
such a stagnant thing wherein every so often some maleficent
and pestilent fly breaks out, or there can arise by chance some
greasy, stinking plant; but instead American Catholicism
is just one more large sect looking for the Happy Hunting
Ground — for virgin lands wherein to make cheerful collec-
tions of unsuspecting souls. It is the sect which postpones
happiness until after death instead of promising it during
life.

Today is Candlemas: the Purification of the Madonna
follows the Purification of the Temple; the candles still
stand in representation of the primitive feast day. People
are most tenacious in maintaining feast days: the myth
changes, but the festival date remains.

Christian art is an expression devoid of meaning, except that which is signified by objects and places of the Christian cult, but then this is no longer an aesthetic distinction. One finds the same art, of the first centuries, in a church, a synagogue, or a pagan temple.

I would like people to have very, very lively bodily instincts but be strictly governed by the power of reason.

February 3, 1931

No "gentleman" can set out to be a painter. Among other things he is hampered by lack of preparation, since in general the great painters have begun to paint or draw at the age of five or six. — What about Whistler? — Whistler was an American "gentleman," not British, which makes a great difference, and then he is not a great painter; artist, yes, but not a great painter. — Ruskin? — No, not Ruskin either: he is a meticulous draftsman, and so seems dazzling to the English, but he is not really a painter. The English have never known how to draw; in terms of all the figurative arts they are children, and feel boundless admiration for those rare compatriots who have learned a little more than the first steps; it is an inoffensive form of nationalism. In England today there are only two painters in any approximative sense: Roger Fry and Ricketts — and how poor they are! Of the less recent, Turner is not a true painter: he never learned to put the human figure together.

It is not true that discussion, or exchange of ideas separated from created works and without direct experience of the works, is a sterile thing; the word is one of the forms of life. And the word passes, whereas the work — no matter what abortion of a work — stays on through the centuries, and is in the best analysis an encumbrance, in the worst an element of corruption for the spirits.

One day a silly and presumptuous young man came here to I Tatti believing that in order to camouflage his timidity he would have to be insolent; he asked for advice, but also firmly announced his own desire to earn his living as a "connoisseur." I said to him: "In all frankness, if you want to make money, don't throw yourself into art criticism, go be a soap manufacturer." Then when he left I accompanied him to the door; it was a gentle and beautiful evening, and in front of the garden full of light the young man, by way of farewell, retorted: "If you had manufactured soap you would not be looking at this spectacular sight today." I could do no less than reply to him: "But I was not born to manufacture soap."

When I was young, at Harvard — I must have been seventeen or eighteen — one day I sat down to read a quantity of Arab poetry by Hafiz, and with amazement saw that love was being addressed to boys. So I asked my professor what this meant, and he — and I don't believe he was being hypocritical — explained to me that in those times it was not permissible to dedicate verses of love to women, so the poets changed the names of their loved ones and pretended to have masculine lovers.

The poetry of the Middle Ages is incredibly boring — after the *Chansons de Geste*, that is to say. One can't understand what pleasure they found in it; it is unexplainable how so much stuff was put together with stanzas and stanzas added to no purpose. Hesiod, at least, even in his dryest moments gives information which he deems useful. One must needs think of a great "commercialism" in the Middle Ages (there are traces of it in the poems themselves) — of a copying monopoly in the monasteries and courts, and of a great deal of time to waste and to occupy.

February 4, 1931

Leconte de Lisle is like a cast of a beautiful bas-relief; when I was young and was filled with a desire to know about the world of India, I found that in reading him there was something which represented it all to me — a not unworthy "ersatz." He also gets that great pomp of the heroicized landscape which one also finds in Flaubert — in all of Flaubert except *Madame Bovary* and parts of the *Education Sentimentale*. Flaubert is superb, but what instinct for self-flagellation leads us to find enjoyment in as dismal a book as *Madame Bovary?*

The memoirs of Bülow will remain as his greatest work; for me they are my impersonal autobiography — much more true than any account of my own experiences. One sees that through the decades all his political activity counts as occasion and material for his memoirs. He is a Prussian nobleman, which defines him as being different from an English or French nobleman of the same period. While the latter felt themselves joint proprietors of their country, that is to say independent, Bülow acts as the employee of a big concern. He was made to be a functionary and therefore not independent. Whoever among them actually had independence was driven mad by it. Sincere? Bülow was sincere; his memoirs were dictated, so he would have been betraying himself had he not been convinced, from one end of the books to the other, of his work and of his manner of presenting it. Not accurate, perhaps, and erroneous in his judgments. For example, he understood nothing about England; but then nobody on the Continent understood the English political situation, that is to say interpreted it as they ought. Russians, French, Germans, Italians might be good interpreters of their reciprocal politics, but they were unfailingly mistaken when they set out to consider the English; they were unable to admit that English politics lacked a plan, a design, that it was entirely fortuitous, and that in being fortuitous it was always ready when the day came. It did not suffer from those provisions and calculations which become prejudices.

Edith Sitwell has a real passion for poetry; when she talks of poetry she has a sense of the musical beauty of words, as she does also when she writes, except that now she is too much accepted by fashion and the current convention; but it is not difficult to abstract from that and to appraise her as she deserves.

February 6, 1931

There is no person disinterested enough to make a fair estimation of any words pronounced in his presence by members of royal families, by princes of the blood. If the princes say "Good morning" everyone cries out in amazement; if they know a date they are credited with profound knowledge and astounding intelligence — or else people react oppositely and every royal word seems low and malicious. Only he who is to the manor born . . .

They are making a great fuss in foreign countries about *Gog*, by Papini. It will be a success among the Germans; the Germans are so good and pious that they will rack their brains to understand what it means and will then write a book about it. — What about the Americans? — No, not the Americans. It will seem to them to be a book of thought, and they don't know how to think.

George Moore is not a person whom I can continue to frequent beyond a certain length of time, because when one enters into an intimate friendship with him he becomes absurd and impossible. He used not to forgive me if I did not invite him to my house whenever I invited other people, and in London it was difficult to find anyone with whom he was not at odds. He is an uncultivated person, but as a writer he incarnates the miracle of style: whatever he touches becomes precious, though not even he knows why. He has his craft at his fingertips, and in this respect differs from the English who do everything as though by a miracle or through simple native talent; it may be because he is Irish, but above all it is because of his Parisian education. Whatever one says, that was a great school: Zola, Maupassant, the Goncourts . . .

Until now England has been governed by the "gentry," but this will not continue — not because it will be replaced, in whatever form, by the proletariat, but because the machinery of state will be more and more augmented and new interests — abstract, technical — will take the upper hand. Bureaucracy in the hands of the experts; this will be the government of the future. The English don't seem to be aware of such a perilous future, but it is to no avail to set too much store by the "innate" qualities of races: I do not believe much in that. There are times in which certain qualities of certain social classes are manifested, and these qualities then become accepted as the necessary and inevitable traits of a whole people. But it is not true. A few circumstances can change and those qualities disappear entirely.

The young should be left alone. They will find their path, but it is natural that once their studies are finished they go for two or three years without knowing what it may be. It is useless to give them financial advice or to worry (financially) on their account. My experience is not great, but it is certainly real: it has shown me that anything done with passion also achieves the necessary remuneration. The pity is when people find themselves struggling with hunger at the outset; for them I feel great compassion.

The memoirs of Bülow are like *The Arabian Nights* for me. People are treated therein each according to his merit. — Isn't he difficult (as a man), choleric and sharp? — But so are all the great: Bismarck, Napoleon, Caesar.

An Irishman who came to Florence as a stable groom was made a Baron by the Grand Duke; when I came here I knew his son, who had pretty well remained an Irish type, and he immediately gave me an exact definition of the Italian character: "We have no reluctance to say what we think," he maintained, "but we hide whatever we feel with great care; the Italians conceal what they think and are not reluctant to externalize what they feel." "However," I answered, "the Irish do show what they feel much more than the English, don't they?" "Certainly, and furthermore they cannot say what they think since they don't think at all."

February 7, 1931

They say that K.P. wants to enter the bosom of the "true religion." But the "true religion" is futuristic; a strange destiny for someone who studies the Middle Ages. Religion looks to the future, only culture looks to the past.

I know what it means to meditate; I always meditate while I am putting on my socks, or if not, when I am finished washing myself in the bath — before I start drying myself. Meditating is "Itting," that is, "getting at it," penetrating to the core. Certainly the problems of the Universe chiefly interest children of five to seven.

Why is it that the Russians, of all the Nordic peoples, are the only ones who know the value of conversation? (In general, the farther north one goes and the more the civilities of custom are chilled, the more the trait of conviviality becomes impoverished.) First of all there is, diffused throughout Russia, a southern element. Then there are those long winter months in the country — countless people gathered indoors with no possibility of leaving.

February 8, 1931

Fakes in sculpture are much easier than fakes in painting. Generally they are not "inventions" of the forgers, but are careful reconstructions of various parts taken from classical models. The Dossena case is more peculiar; it cannot be the result of any activity of his own, nor of the advice of antique dealers, who never arrive at such erudite subtlety by themselves. Some critic or other must have given him the idea of "creating" the sculpture of Simone Martini; only a critic, a connoisseur, a person of erudition, could conceive the idea of translating the most anti-plastic of painters into sculpture. That an inspiration of that type could come naturally cannot even be considered. One who has a practice in restoring old paintings throws himself at more modern things if he wants to paint on his own. Only a great technician of painting, with modern sensibilities, can approach possession of the ancient technique and "remake" things in the style of the great masters; which is the case of Roger Fry, who has done it as a game.

Positive criticism and negative criticism: adjectives which have no meaning. The critic must be an illuminator, nothing else. In England, for ten or twenty years, they have left off believing in criticism and therefore have assumed an attitude of greater tolerance — critical Pyrrhonism — the attitude one takes toward things of no importance. Aesthetic problems are not important to any Englishman, nor are many other problems, outside of political matters, so an Englishman will only get excited over these. I consider it a great evil. It is Bloomsbury's fault: they have made (criticism) the province of a clique, conferring on it a dandyism which now affects everyone. Thus my very dear brother-in-law, Logan Pearsall Smith, cannot bear to hear of a critic who takes his profession seriously, like Lucas. Criticism conducted in this fashion is the death of taste.

The turgid mask of Bernanos . . .

The members of the French aristocracy never stop maligning the Germans, holding them responsible for everything villainous, and considering them monsters in human dress. They do not budge from their own positions, largely because they have no part in "affairs," and yet nonetheless they manage to produce a malicious effect because they are imitated by the whole "snob" world, whose attitude is then worse (if possible) than the French in that it does not possess the conviction. During the war there were military men and diplomats who did not believe in the "sales Boches" and saw clearly into the future and even feared for their victory; intellectuals saddened by the lies and propaganda who did not dare to speak, but there was not a single man of "high society" who was not a born informer and a "bourreur de crâne."

Psychoanalysts are not occupied with the minds of their patients; they do not believe in the mind but in a cerebral intestine.

The American government, with its provision for "Deadlock" (the possibility of insoluble disagreement between the legislative and executive powers) is a fine system of government, preventing those who govern from doing that little evil and that great good which they would like. It is the good intentions of people who govern which are considerably the more dangerous.

February 9, 1931

Academicism is not a necessary result of the study of masterpieces. Tiepolo never painted from nature, but re-examined all his artistic subjects with a concave eye which embraced figures, air and landscape all together. The Carracci are academicians: I mean to say they "compose" their paintings of various exemplary fragments and do not take their figures as a whole — the heads and hands are "models" in themselves, disconnected; even their portraits are mediocre; they lack interpretation. Any Florentine mannerist whatever — Salviati, for example — is better than they are.

The most profound intelligences can be the most credulous, if they lack what I call "antecedent probability." This applies to the minds of Americans. Their upbringing, their studies, their culture has not prepared them to know how to distinguish the probable from the improbable, and they are ready to believe everything, to become inflamed by everything. They have no preventive limitations, which would be a great safeguard. The American mentality is convex: things escape and bounce off from all sides, which is a sign of lack of civilization, since civilization also means that sense of the possible which is acquired through a well-digested tradition.

Whitehead and Santayana: the "tone" of these two philosophers is not only dissimilar, but is, indeed, opposed. Whitehead says very profound things — both just and intelligent — but it then escapes the reader how they are brought together, to what they all refer; Santayana speaks at length in clear and subtle discourse, but one senses right away that he is spinning around in the void, that it is a perfect logomachia.

Ancient Chinese lyrics, in Waley's translations, express everything directly, without rhetorical gyrations or ornamental imagery. The primitive Greek lyrics, by Sappho or Alcmaeon, were like this. Richness of imagery comes from the epic, and from tragedy.

February 10, 1931

When the French speak of "Pan-Europe" they mean all of Europe under French domination.

Instead of writing a novel, J. E. Blanche should have been the Vasari of the nineteenth century; French painting of the last century is as important as the Florentine painting of the Renaissance. As a painter, Blanche is a good iconographer, but he is not a photographic painter because photography is not essentially good iconography. Raeburn or Gainsborough are true painters, though we cannot say how "photographic" they are — that is, how true their portraits are to the originals — because we lack knowledge of the originals from other sources. Raeburn in particular, who painted rough, thickset Scottish types, is a good painter, the only Englishman who knew about "tactile values."

February 11, 1931

The ideal biography for most readers is that in which the loves and the broken love affairs of the people in question are recounted; their habits, and the pattern of their home life, what time they go to bed, that at 2 A.M. they pay a visit to their wife (or to their mistress), that then they take a purge, go to the bathroom, and return to work well rested the next morning. Exaggeration of the Saint-Beuvian biography. I on the other hand, who spend so few words on each artist and give so little information, cannot hope to be either loved or read.

The one form of bad manners which the English have, particularly the young ones, is remaining silent in the midst of other people. Everything can be hidden behind silence: timidity, arrogance, virtue, vice. It is an unpleasant defect, because the presence of a person cannot be ignored. Every human presence makes an impression on me, so that for my own part I cannot stand by quietly, and ask no questions.

February 12, 1931

It is not possible to maintain that Sicilian art of the Middle Ages is directly derived from classical art without any Byzantine influence. Everything that was done in those centuries passed through Byzantium — not necessarily through Byzantium the place, but through the spirit, the culture, of Byzantium. As for local artistic creativity in Sicily, it does not seem to me that there is anything, not even as little, clumsy and rough as it is, as that which flowered in Calabria with the Basilian Fathers . . . It is not true that in Byzantine art the figures are always "empty"; there are full forms, and there is a sense of volume . . . If there are some "evaporated," poorly defined forms, tending to meld into the background and fade away, such as Cimabue's forms, there are also the much more contained, more definite forms of Cavallini. Miss A., who would you consider the more Byzantine of the two? — Oh, Cimabue. — There, I've caught you. If you study him deeply you will see that one by one all the elements that are found in Cavallini are also found in the thirteenth century in Byzantium, in Greece, in Novgorod, in Kiev. Believe me, in all the years that I have been studying this problem, I am increasingly convinced that Byzantium is at the root of all the art which has evolved in our western world, up to and including Lorenzo Monaco. In sculpture it is the same story: at the foundation of our medieval sculpture are the Byzantine ivories; what little Sicilian sculpture there is can be reduced to ivories enlarged and adapted to different materials, nothing more. I challenge you to prove to me that the capitals of Monreale are medieval. Either they precede the fourth century, or they are Renaissance (at the most, one of the uglier could be a clumsy imitation of the other classical capitals done in the Middle Ages to fill the gaps). Medieval workmanship is unmistakable: look at the bust in the Museum in Capua, what an awkward thing it is, though it is nevertheless pleasing because it is sincere. Only in the Renaissance was the classical really "recreated" because then the spirit returned more closely to the classical, as did manual ability. To distinguish between the sculptures of the sixteenth century and those of the first centuries it is not enough to have a taste for it and an eye; one needs a knowledge of the technical minutiae, of the material and of the way it is treated. The Monreale capitals could have been taken from any ruined monument — Sicily must have been full of them. Probably from the portico of a palace, rather than from a temple. What do we know of that time? There was no Touring Guide, there wasn't even a Pausanius for Sicily. Five centuries of Romanesque Sicily have left no record: which means that they were a happy and prosperous people. Panormo was a large city, and perhaps there were other monuments which rose out of the surrounding countryside. For the rest, you study this problem, Miss A.; I only ask that any scholar arrive at his "own" conclusions, so long as he reach them after having seen all there is to see, being fully informed, and being free of nationalistic-cultural prejudices, which are dreadful.

As far as this question of Byzantium goes, I certainly have no prejudices or preferences, and it is after much much study that I have resolved to acknowledge the Byzantine influence.

One should read the last book of Gorki's memoirs in order to understand what sort of people the "kulaks" are — extremely cruel to anyone subordinate to them, and, what is worse, monopolists of the money in the countryside, and therefore born usurers and responsible for all the miseries of the poor. Today's measures against the "kulaks" certainly have the approval of all the peasants. The cruelty of the Russians, and Bolshevism itself, are explained by the fact that Russia is in a medieval state; all of Europe was cruel in the Middle Ages, and it took many centuries for the cruelty to pass, but Russia has remained firmly in that state, and in any moment of crisis she reveals herself as barbarian. The tendency to abolish private property is natural in a country which has never believed in it, which has never seriously tried it out, which still retains a nomadic frame of mind. The great lords were still virtually encamped on their territories, and depended for their well-being on the grace of the Czar. As for religion, one would have thought it should have been much more deeply rooted in the hearts of the Russian people. Cer-

tainly it was its link with power which produced its down-
fall, and besides, the religious impulse of the people turned
to hatred. The love of the "humiliated and wronged" (which
in any case is more Dostoevskian than Russian) is not such
a singular phenomenon: it is one facet of Christianity, inherited from Byzantium. Russia is extremely Greco-Byzan-
tine. Rasputin bears this out.

How can we ever understand anything about China?
First of all we would have to remember the names of the
towns and the important people and know how to recognize
them. But it is strange that a country which has such a lively
history of art and literature should continue to be so chaotic
and cruel.

February 13, 1931
   The architecture of those German cities which have not
been destroyed (and this means almost all) is one of the
most harmonious things one can imagine. One shouldn't
seek it out in overly tourist centers like Rothenburg, nor
even perhaps Nuremberg, but in the infinite number of other
small and rarely frequented cities. French architecture is
more beautiful, but not the English. Salisbury Cathedral is
perfect, but perfect in the same way as a model which has
been enlarged to normal proportions without a single un-
predictable element, and without any surprises.

King Milan of Serbia was renowned as a swindler. One day
he was gambling with a Jewish banker and was losing and

losing. At a certain point he said: "Vous allez me manger vivant." "Sire, ma religion me le défend." [1]

The Germans are the people who best know how to bear "l'ennui auguste." They are never aware of being bored, which is to say they are never bored, so things can happen to them which we could not even dream of. We, being prey to boredom, miss great sensations which would only occur if one persisted for a long while in one certain direction.

The Tale of Genji is not remote from me — it is perhaps closer to me than any other novel. It is a great symphony of love. One feels, on the part of everyone in it, a continuous homage to beauty; even if one realizes that for some of them it is a pose, a verbal ceremony, that they feign some sentiments and not others, it is still a most revealing index of the culture of a society. It really treats of the most refined society I know — people "in the clouds," who only give in to life when it is a purely physiological matter. And it is a society as much without violence as it is without real ambition. Feudal violence begins when that world has already died, like our Middle Ages after the civilization of the third and fourth centuries. In other literatures only one book resembles it: *La Princesse de Clèves,* but it is much shorter.

February 14, 1931

The English have established the law of dressing in the evening as an excellent revenge on everyday reality. That

---

[1] "You are going to eat me alive." "Sire, my religion forbids it."

quarter of an hour which each man spends on his own toilet is the secret of great rest and of great comfort; it separates all annoyances, business, and worries from the evening.

It is every reviewer's duty to set down clearly the argument of the book he is discussing. A reader does not ask anything more; and if he then puts his criticism into play, it will be very much better founded with the support of a good summary of the book itself. — Even the reviewer of a novel? — Yes, only he can do better by filling out the résumé of the story with personal criticisms and observations. Now if a young man wants to express his aesthetic ideas in a critical work I would always advise him to wait twenty years, because then, very probably, he would not dare express them because he would no longer have them. — But didn't you say that twenty was the best age to devote oneself to criticism? — To write criticism, yes. Not to invent an aesthetic; between twenty and twenty-five is the age at which one has the most faith in one's own ideas, and at which one applies oneself most fervently to what one reads.

Something is lacking in Davidsohn which keeps him from being a perfect historian. He still represents the heroic type of documentary researcher, one of those who can never forget a single thing they have known or discovered; the prerogative of memory, on the other hand, is to forget, but at that time they didn't know that. Thus Creighton, another one, wrote his wonderful history and then in an appendix published two little documents which were barely relevant but which for him justified the whole work. In Davidsohn's work the collecting of facts, the interpretation, and even the synthesis of the thought is all perfect, but he does not know how to present things as a writer — to discriminate between them. Italians accuse him of writing a history of Florence which is too Ghibelline, but this is not fair. For him it is not "patriotic history," it is universal history. That is, an Italian would ordinarily be struck first by the history of the Guelf Commune in Florence. Davidsohn, on the other hand, sees and narrates the history which is characteristic of that day *in* Florence, as though it had been studied and observed in Florence. This is his Ghibellinism.

February 15, 1931

What there is of Tuscan jewelry in the Renaissance is extremely fine, above all the saltcellar by Cellini in Vienna. It is a shame that a lack of richness should have occurred so quickly; by 1520 the Florentines already could no longer compete with Germany. From then on the style of jewelry deteriorated increasingly, and certainly in the last century it was at its lowest level.

The worst period for feminine fashions was from 1870 to '80. I remember having suffered as a child from the presence of people without knowing why; and now I understand that it was because of the fashion. It forced ladies to look like ostriches. The best eras in fashion are those in which one is least tempted to mask the human body; since the war the effect has been excellent. Also Greek fashions, and those of the

Napoleonic Empire. Renaissance clothes were very ugly, with that iron prison of a bodice, and the Middle Ages are not very satisfying (though it is true that we only see ceremonial costumes depicted) because the stuffs are too hard and pompous.

Is the new Antonello da Messina genuine?[1] What Moroni says counts up to a certain point: it could well be that the painting seemed to be by Cavazzola before the cleaning and that then afterwards it appeared to be a true Antonello. And nobody denies that Moroni must have worked hard on it; at times, in restoration, there remains only half a face, and any conscientious restorer turns to the experts to find out what to do about the missing parts; they in turn refer him, for sources of information, to other paintings by similar masters or by the same supposed master. Frizzoni saw the picture first, but he is dead and cannot speak; he considered it extremely good before restoration. De Nicola brought it to me, long after Adolfo Venturi's publication. The authority of both rendered me prejudicially favorable, but had it been false I would have realized it from the reproduction, even before examining it. The fact that only 100 lire was paid for it has no significance; the best paintings here at I Tatti did not cost any more. It could well be that at first the painting seemed to be a Cavazzola, but, if you think about it, how do you "make" an Antonello out of a Cavazzola? How can you say it is "easy" to change a Cavazzola into an Antonello?

[1] This refers to a "Bust of a Friar," first in the Chiesa collection in Milan, then in the Cambó collection in Barcelona, now (1961) in the Museum of Catalan Art in Barcelona (Cambó bequest).

I know ten or twenty painters who could be "Antonellized" but not Cavazzola, who has something about him like Spagna, or a weak Perugino. Antonello has that primitive force that Egyptian primitives have. It would make more sense to speak in terms of a complete fake — but then why do it on a board which already had a Cavazzola painted on it? Better to use any piece of old wood. And then who is there who would ever know how to make an Antonello that was so much an Antonello — one which was not a copy of any other known Antonello, and yet could rank among the most beautiful Antonellos? When I saw it, the impression was excellent, and for twenty years I have never been mistaken in a first impression. Sometimes careful examination has made me doubt a fake which at first glance had seemed obvious to me, but not vice versa; and in general the facts have always borne out my first reaction. A radiograph would give reliable results because it would reveal the first draft, the first stage of the painting, but this would not necessarily be the same as the finished picture. Antonello first drew or painted the figure in front of him, then went over it idealizing it; but I guess I can tell right from the first drawing whether or not it is an Antonello. Chemical tests do not prove anything; they test colors as one would test human blood, "puncturing" in one or two places, and by chance, or perhaps by malice aforethought, they are apt to hit exactly on the retouched spots, in which any painting abounds no matter how good a condition it may be in. The only painting in a pristine state which I know was Botticelli's "Birth of Venus" before it made the trip to London. If it be proved that Antonello's

Friar is false, it means that nobody can any longer guarantee a painting which has not issued from the hand of the artist under his very eyes.

February 16, 1931

I would like to call Duccio a great Byzantine painter. I could show photographs of beautiful Byzantine things and say they were works by Duccio, and perhaps not more than two or three people would recognize the deception. The Byzantine civilization was very strong in Italy too, and took on new vigor at the end of the fourteenth century, as shown by Lorenzo Monaco, that is to say before the coming of Emperor Paleologus, who came to Italy poor and miserable and was unable to promote the diffusion of art. The Byzantine court during the fourteenth century sold as much as it could; there is for example the beautiful manuscript in the Libreria Pubblica in Siena, whose acquisition was entrusted to a Sienese friar sent for the purpose to Venice, where this manuscript had been sent specifically for solicitation of its sale.

February 17, 1931

The greatest miracle I saw at Lourdes was that I began to bawl like a calf, and if I hadn't been hardheaded that day I would have fallen down and worshiped and one of the most extraordinary conversions would have taken place. In a world which is so full of lurid concerns, it is a superhuman thing to hear the cry of hope. What difference does it make if the healings are not genuine? Poor humanity believes itself healed and rejoices with exceeding great joy. The "mise en

scène" of the Church sometimes beats Diaghileff or Rein-
hardt, because it seems so natural; all the gimmicks are hidden. The architecture is ugly, but it comes to life in the pro-
cessions up and down the terraces and staircases, made
especially for sacred demonstrations and for the genuflec-
tions of the faithful.

The contrast between the countryside of Pau and Spain,
as you cross the Pyrenees at Canfranc, is the greatest that
one can imagine. On one side the landscape of Europe —
almost tropical in the abundance of its vegetation, fertile,
fruitful, pregnant with cultivation — and, on the other side,
Africa — untended and barren.

To conduct technical research in order to arrive at the
"perfection" of the ancients in their pictorial processes is an
absurdity. Nobody can expect to express himself outside of
his current language. The masters of the Renaissance are not
appropriate examples, in that they sought to relive the spirit
of the ancient world, not to imitate its techniques. Theirs
was a romantic passion for antiquity which they expressed
in their paintings through a pictorial language contemporary
to them. Raphael, certainly, knew many ancient works,
works which are lost by now, but probably he didn't take
much notice of the colors; they did inspire him, but only in
the sense I have mentioned.

The young art student M. S. is the typical Talmudic
scholar: he knows an infinite number of minute particulars
and can never forget them; for this reason he asphyxiates me.

March 4, 1931

Is Croce's clarity exaggerated? Clarity always comes at the expense of many other things; it is reached by dint of discarding. Perhaps I am partial in my admiration of him (when I do admire him) because he is the spokesman of a world which is dear to me, and of ideas for which I consider myself one of the most authorized representatives — those of true liberalism. In writing to him, I have begged him to explain why on earth liberalism has had, in recent history, such a short life span, passing by so quickly to be transformed into nationalism, or into imperialism, which are the ideologies most opposed to it. Croce's recent essays certainly are polemical in a profound sense; he feels called upon to combat any ideas which are contrary to his, but he tries to seek out whatever rationale may be residing in them. The Oxford Lecture is antifascist, but not in the usual and immediate sense of the word, since it is not directed at the political actions of Fascism but at all the fascism spreading through the world, at the universal "forma mentis" which encourages it and of which it is a product. I don't read Croce the philosopher because I have no faith in philosophy; I read the historian, and I consider him a great historian. But like every true historian he has a tendency to overestimate the "necessity" of the things which happen. This necessity does, in a sense, exist, since they are rings in a chain and cannot be detached, but in another sense one surely could do without many of the rings. — Cannot error, or rather something which at a certain moment seems erroneous, often be a source of good? — Yes, but error also kills, and in history there is an enormous amount of waste.

I Capricci dell'Adriana by that nice young Bonsanti is too much a descriptive work and does not move forward in any definite direction; the epoch in which it has been placed is too vague, that is to say not even the author seems to believe in it. Placing stories in a bygone epoch need not mean that it be historically reconstructed, but the author must demonstrate that he does believe in it — in whatever has been created out of his imagination. This is an appealing story for the pleasant jocundity to which one returns after delving into so many horrors, but the narrative is not conducted as it ought to be. On many counts it is a youthful work.

I have read *Urto dei Simili* (by Bino Sanminiatelli) with pleasure. It is not a novel, it is not a book whose issues are resolved, but it certainly contains characters, and offers the representation of a society which no longer believes in itself: a bad, but truthful sign.

March 5, 1931

The art of Mediterranean Africa during the Roman Empire is interesting because it represents a stage of transition which can explain the Spanish art which followed. The Ashburnham manuscript (a Bible) from the fifth and sixth centuries is a pre-Byzantine Spanish work which one cannot understand without considering it as having African paternity; this being found, to the best of our knowledge so far, in third and fourth century mosaics. The third century was a golden age for Mediterranean Africa, contributing emperors and writers to Rome, and saints, theologians and think-

ers to the Church, so its artistic manifestations naturally must
have been powerful. They were "variants" of the Aegean
art which from there went on to spread first to Rome and
later to Byzantium. Alexandria functioned in the way that
New York functions today: the center of resonance, the
monopolist of artistic activities. Much of what we call Alexandrian art must really have come from the rest of Africa.

As a type of architecture, for anyone who would like to
construct a dwelling today, I would advise the little Larderel
palace, on Via Tornabuoni in Florence. Being almost without
particular style and without epoch it is reproducible without the resulting building's being obviously "modeled" on
it. Whoever seeks to achieve something beautiful in architecture is certain to obtain something ugly as the result; but
let the internal function of the building determine the lines,
and everything will go well. In America up until 1850 the
word "beauty" was unknown except as a sign of diabolic
perversion, and they constructed very decent buildings;
later they sought to imitate the different "styles" and the
horrors began. A skyscraper city is beautiful to see as a
whole, as scenic decoration, but not as architecture. Then
there are certain efforts by modern architects which are
nothing more than the reconstruction of buildings painted
by painters as backgrounds in their pictures. When I took
part in a commission for the construction of a new bridge on
the Grand Canal, in place of the iron bridge at the Accademia,
the models I saw all seemed to me to be copies of bridges by
Guardi.

The art of the storyteller is quite different from "being able to write." Whether or not he writes badly or pedestrianly, Walter Scott is nevertheless a prodigious storyteller. The English do have it in the highest degree; and are also excellent historians; one reads even the most puerile English books with attention because of this quality. But why is it found so seldom in Italian literature? It's true that sometimes one meets it: in Manzoni, for example, and above all in Boccaccio. Boccaccio's writing is not very agile — anybody today writes better than he, and many write better than Manzoni — but they do not even know where narrative belongs. If a book is well "told" one eagerly begins reading it, and later goes on to evaluate its other qualities.

March 6, 1931

D'Annunzio would have been an extraordinary man had he not had two enormous defects: living a sort of false ideal of the adventurous life, taking all that went with it — wine, women and song — ridiculously seriously; and approaching all forms of art with tremendous dandyism.

Music, it is true, he felt more sincerely, but only old music; modern music, Wagner for example, provided him with a pretext for life, like all the rest. It would have been a noteworthy fact to have known D'Annunzio at Pescara, with his mother, who must have been a sweet woman, living in a comfortable old house without any pretenses. His father damaged him, with the usual familial obtuseness, by not putting any sort of stop to the precocious exploitation of his gifts, and he was also damaged by the heartfelt applause of several critics, Nencioni being chief among them. Nencioni was an extremely acute connoisseur of foreign literature who, however, had stopped short with the writers who were "the latest thing" in his early youth (he never could accept my being chary in my admiration for Browning) and who only caught fire again at the sound of D'Annunzio's voice.

If Du Bos had accepted my invitation to come stay here with us this winter he would have felt uneasy because he cannot live without a nucleus of listeners to whom he pontificates. He is trivial, and is most solemn in his triviality. He has a brain but does not know how to use it, sinking into swamps of one kind or another from which he sees will-o'-the-wisps flash out and thinks they are glorious lights — stars of the first magnitude.

Dear Sessions,[1] L. gets angry with you because you do not make any "concessions to beauty" in your music. Beauty, for him, means the troubadours' serenades.

March 7, 1931

The Vatican is a kind of shameless Tammany Hall which has lasted for nineteen centuries. I am not saying, however, that with this disparaging definition I am completely exhausting the concept of what the Vatican represents. But each time I have had anything to do with it it has been as though I entered into a cellar and stumbled into a mass of spiderwebs.

1 Roger Sessions, the American composer.

It is not the moral sense which is lacking in Italians, but the political sense; if we take a typical average Italian like De F. we really can't say that he lacks the moral sense. The lack, in any case, does not stem from the Counter-Reformation, which was also produced by moral forces (the moral demands of Protestantism were all taken up by the Counter-Reformation); it is not an effect of the reborn "pagan era" of the fifteenth century, which was only pagan in some people and was in reality a continual flowering both of religious movements and rebirths and of heresies, all guided by enlightened spirits from the middle class and the more thinking element of the aristocracy. Rather it was in the last century that the Italians were anachronistic, in having resolved a problem — liberation from the foreigner — which was not felt by the rest of the world and which distracted them from the internal problems of liberty, of personal dignity, and of true modern political relationships. Their struggle against the "tyrant" from outside has kept them from seeing the possibility of tyranny, or of a tyrannical class, from within. Foreign domination is not always, in every case, deplorable: Franche-Comté produced good Frenchmen before it ended up under the scepter of the king of France (an undertaking, however, which was personally, not nationally, monarchic); Savoy up to recent days was French in customs and in sentiment, although faithful to the House of Savoy. Today, perhaps, secure in her natural boundaries, with the specter of the foreign enemy removed, Italy will learn to hold dear those other aspects of well-being which she has heretofore overlooked.

Hindus' book on Russia is philobolshevik in an aesthetic sense; at least what appears uniquely in the clarity of his portrayal is the reality of Russia animated by hope and reaching out toward the future, and in that it is convincing — even moving. It is objective in its manner of recalling the past — the very free, idyllic life of the Cossacks, for example — and in indicating the benefits which were lost and the pain which was suffered, and this objectivity also serves to bring out the struggle and the passion of today more vividly.

Wuthering Heights is explainable in English literature as a souvenir of the epic Icelandic sagas of the tenth and twelfth centuries. The Brontës are typical representatives of the Scandinavian colonists, who have comparable descendants in Sweden with Selma Lagerlöf. *Gösta Berling* is a repetition of the same powerful sense of nature — that density of atmosphere and that passion in the characters.

March 8, 1931

American Senators: I don't know even one, but I love them all cordially. They are, of all legislative bodies, the body which is most effective in obstructing tyranny. The executive power in America is held in check by the Senate; that is, the field is left open for it to execute the law but not to dictate it. And my political convictions, like my historical convictions, give me a predilection for an impotent executive power — impotent to do whatever great harm or little good it would be able to do if it were not controlled.

Pedantry grows out of a shallow intelligence which has no ability in mastering culture.

Moravia is indifferent to the things that are around him, therefore he will never "improve" from countries that he sees or from experiences he may have. He lacks a sense of humor, but instead possesses in the highest degree a sense of the absurdity of things, and this may make him laugh, but more often it leads him to a sense of the tragic. He perceives reality clearly, and more than anyone else is capable of indignation: moral indignation and political indignation, like a Hebrew prophet — a rare thing in Italy and something which predisposes me in his favor.

When the intellectual class is not turbulent it means that there is not much life in a nation. The perpetual insurgence of its intellectuals, even if absurd, is a good sign for Spain.

In my long life I am persuaded that the most idiotic people govern and the most vulgar people rule, whom one can possibly imagine.

All the American soldiers who disembarked in France received a pamphlet on the first page of which was written: "Think of your mother, think of your country, think of the respect you owe to yourself, and BE PURE, but if you can't resist, turn over and read these instructions."

June 12, 1931

Are there really any cities larger than a village? I often think of New York as a collection of hostile wigwams.

June 13, 1931

If a woman keeps silent intelligently her company is precious. Those who only know how to speak intelligently speak too much; the moment comes when they drive us mad with an out-of-place observation, with an impertinent question, with an asinine interruption. Perhaps we love them even in these unpleasant moments, because they convince us of our superiority.

Guido Reni has always attracted me by his quality of extreme coldness — in being a glacial, arctic painter: "The Massacre of the Innocents," "Atalanta and Hippomenes." The portrait of his mother is a lovely thing, and I fell in love with it after having already seen and understood his other pictures, almost through amazement that he could achieve a likeness of that quality while keeping himself pure and cold. The true portraits are those by Sebastiano del Piombo or Bronzino; in Guido Reni's portraits there is already a new, lesser reflection — that of intimacy.

The Carracci are great producers; they flood the market, and they are the most typical academicians of all, and yet, with their best efforts they do succeed in doing accomplished works, like the frescoed Gallery of the Farnese Palace.

One would do well to study Guido Reni and Guercino together. If one did a history of seventeenth century paintings, using the criteria with which I have written about the Renaissance, one would have to treat them as being united. I wish that the history of art would be "depersonalized" — that people would not lose themselves in biographical research of miniscule particularities and in attributions, but would seek to plot the "curve," the "evolutionary parabola" of painting in the great works of art. Titian and Giorgione should be considered together. Whoever has set out to write about the seventeenth century has always "revenged" the century against critics and against preceding painters, as if one couldn't praise one artist without slandering another.

Another important artistic problem: what prepared the way for Poussin? There were the Carracci, and Domenichino enters in; thanks to them landscape begins to live, not function solely as a background for figures.

There was a polemical reason for my writing my books; not so much the need to oppose Ruskin, who was a genius, but to oppose the followers of Ruskin — those who judged a picture according to its abstract subject. For this reason I tried to exaggerate the importance of the hitherto neglected pictorial qualities, with the result that whoever has read me has, in his turn, exaggerated my intentions, and from my moderate disapproval of the "illustrative" quality of painting, has derived a cubist aesthetic.

I have never come across any painters who knew how to judge and appreciate art, because painters in general are blind to everything except that aspect of technique which interests them. They don't believe that problems can be serious unless they represent an especial difficulty for them. The one exception was Matisse. Matisse, with hard, Norman logic, understood everything, and continued to understand until the moment when he became a fad producer, at the service of every momentary vogue, even of Marie Laurencin.

"Color" is a term which serves to confuse ideas. Color reigns less in painting than anywhere else. One must seek out a colored surface in the painted panels of the eighteenth century, in the lacquered carriages of the beginning of the nineteenth century, and for color combinations one looks to rugs. In painting, color acts as form, in the chiaroscuro, in its passage from dark to light. A drawing or a charcoal sketch is painting as much as any painted picture. Besides, I would like to say something paradoxical: Rembrandt's engravings, like his late paintings, are not painting but sculpture; for me Rembrandt is the Donatello of his century. And likewise there are sculptures which are all light and shadow — essentially pictorial.

Titian paints the fullness of summer, and Bellini the high skies above the sea.

June 14, 1931
Berthelot[1] is typical of the "grand commis"; aristocracy

1 Philippe Berthelot, a high official in the French Foreign Ministry at the time.

in bureaucracy, with the nationalistic ideals of the Ancien Régime modernized and made wiser. He and the two Cambons have sustained French diplomacy in this century. Briand does not "sustain" anything. He is too lazy and lackadaisical.

June 15, 1931

Maeterlinck is not a poet, he is a "parfumeur verbaliste."

One evening, during one of Madame Narishkine's dinners during the heyday of Florence in the first part of the twentieth century, when Mansuroff was still alive and the tall skinny Liechtenstein acted as her paramour, Liechtenstein asked me if I would be going to Bruges, where the Golden Fleece was on exhibit. The Count of Turin, with a start, interrupted the conversation: "Bruges? qu'est-ce que c'est que Bruges?" and Liechtenstein answered: "Monseigneur plaisante; Monseigneur sait bien que je veux parler de l'admirable ville flamande que tout le monde aime et connaît." [1] When dinner was finished the Count of Turin followed the ladies out of the dining room with Liechtenstein immediately behind; on the threshold the Count turned around to him and pointing at him in front of all the bystanders exclaimed: "Grand savant."

The Count of Turin was so accustomed to drilling in the Piazza d'Armi that, when he was out walking, he would repeat to himself: "one, two, one, two" to keep step, like the Duc d'Angoulême.

[1] "Bruges? What is Bruges?" . . . "Your Highness is joking; Your Highness knows perfectly well that I wish to speak of the admirable Flemish city which all the world knows and loves."

If something does not go well, no matter what it is (like Ojetti's visit today) I feel that it is all my fault, and I never can manage to blame anyone else.

June 16, 1931

Mary[1] has ruined my life by inducing me to write books. If I had not written books what would I have become? I would have become a true gentleman.

Nicholas M. Butler (President of Columbia University) is vain and fatuous, but he is no fool, and he does try to popularize the ideas which are dear to him. One can make, with respect to his actions, the same comment that Bourget made about England. It was the first year of the war and I was trying to convince Bourget to be more kindly toward the English who, after all, had saved France. "Oui, oui, tout ce que vous voulez, mon cher ami, rien pourtant ne m'empêche de considérer l'Angleterre perfide. Mais puisque la perfidie est avec nous . . ."[2]

I would like to reverse the usual expression and say: "any friends of our friends are NOT our friends." I have found some of the most awful people among friends of the people most dear to me. — But isn't it possible to feel that some of one's own friends are awful, yet they are friends all the same? — No, not that. But one can love certain friends the way one loves a plate of food, despite the fact that there

---

[1] Mary Berenson, Bernard's wife.
[2] "Yes, yes, anything you like, my dear friend, but nothing can keep me from considering England perfidious. But since perfidy is on our side . . ."

may be too much seasoning or sauce — too much flavor — so that one loves the substance but not the taste. Certainly at first new friends are apt to be "the friends of friends"; it is difficult to meet them by chance (for instance the ghastly dilemma: "He is in love with his best friend's wife." How could he have managed to fall in love with his particular enemy's wife?). But it is when we have already become established and secure friends that we find we are amazed by our friends' friends. This happens because we are all polygonal beings, and we only reveal one side of ourselves to each of our friends. That is to say nobody really exists in himself, but exists through encounters with others; everyone differs according to his various friendships. Every person I meet acts on me like the moon on the sea. Benefactors of humanity, philanthropists, public officials, are most apt to be "consistent." True friendship, as distinguished from simple loyalty in human relationships, lies in this mutual mobility of the spirit.

June 17, 1931

In novels we cannot "recognize" scenes, persons and facts from life except in the case that caricature exposes them on purpose. Literature does not permit "interpretations" when it is good literature. It transforms reality and is created out of imagination.

June 18, 1931

The Church in Spain has the presumption of a raging lion — it is not a little sheep with a blue ribbon around its neck, it is an organism which is continually alive and violent and I do not find this in the least unpleasant. But by doing this it does offend people — even the souls of the faithful — and turns them to anticlericalism, so that every fifty or sixty years insurrections occur like those of these last few days. It has the same aspect and arrogance as the German army before the war. That finished badly, but the Spanish people are too profoundly Catholic, even when they rebel, to cut themselves off from the Church, and Catholicism — even Spanish Catholicism — will always find the manner and formula for staying alive no matter how much conditions may differ from those when it is predominant.

I remember that the day of the murder at Sarajevo I was taking tea with J. E. Blanche and a lady arrived who had innumerable connections. Without greeting anyone, she said: "There is terrible news; they have assassinated the Archduke." For a minute everyone was struck dumb. Then, not even the inflamed discussions of those first days were as alarming as the silence which followed: a deathly silence, in which one felt the presentiment of what was about to happen.

Though not responsible for it in the moral sense, one "cause" of the war was Sir Edward Grey's attitude during that whole month. No one detested it more than he, and no one contributed more to precipitating it. In the same way, on the other side, the will of the German army precipitated it, in absolutely refusing to waste that opportunity — in being possessed by true "hubris," like the Russian army, which had learned nothing from the Russo-Japanese War and was incapable of evaluating anything. The German army was "hubristic" — arrogant and sure of itself — but the French army was not. Fear has dominated France from the eighteenth century on, and even since the war the knowledge of having won through Allied help makes everything into politics of defense for them.

June 19, 1931

After the war the French had a genius for mendicity. Economically they had not suffered much, yet they found ways of being given enormous sums of money by the richer Allies. They also had a genius for intrigue: the loan which they obtained almost at the historic par value of the franc in relation to gold, and which they obtained right away in 1919 after great propaganda, represents a deliberate proposal to deceive — to obtain money from everyone before inflation started which would reduce the debt by three quarters. The Germans, on the other hand, probably had no desire for bankruptcy, but when they saw that there was no help for it, they could also see that its consequences might not be altogether damaging.

No political opinion is more treacherous (in its optimism) than that of the financier bankers with regard to the states financed by them. Classic examples from before the war: Russia and Mexico, in whom blind faith was advocated by everyone. People like Lamont always had predilections for the most shattered states of all, and embarked on preferential negotiations with the least secure governments because they were the most obliging. Such states are always sure to be able to settle their affairs before everything goes to rack and ruin because they save themselves from danger just in time by unloading themselves on minor or private organizations. There is great immorality at the basis of this practice, though it is hidden (in Anglo-Saxons) by all the possible justifications — even evangelical.

The Italian army is as disciplined as any other, but, except in Piedmont, it lacks a long tradition. One could say that in the other regions of the country people are "superior" to the military type, being intimately tied to their work and to the prosperity of peace. The standards of militarism, therefore, represent barbarization to the Italians.

June 20, 1931

I cannot stand the convention of breaking the rhythm of verse graphically by writing it out in little scraps. All verse — all the "forms" of art — are a convention, and require great genius to make them classical rather than conventional. The first person to invent terza rima conquered a new realm for poetry. Edgar Lee Masters took a great deal from Greek anthologies, but also knew how to represent American life as an epic.

— Is it true now that X.Y., who was so promising as a youth, runs the danger of becoming like any other typical American of his class? — It is true. I have seen many of them — young, perceptive, vibrant people, open to any idea — become crystallized as soon as they went back to America, changing into heavy, sluggish, snobbish men, closed and adverse to anything new. The one cure for them is to stay in Europe and not return until the age of forty. (Another risk though, even to staying in Europe, is that of losing their own "weight" and their own importance by surrendering to a sort of frivolity of intellect, like my brother-in-law Logan.) In the first place, no matter what the time, there is the danger that everything be absorbed by society: the mighty "baronial" American society which is actually a society of peasants, raised within three generations to extreme power in wealth and social domination. X.Y., who really is still free, already shows certain tendencies, certain kernels in his thinking around which his whole intellectual life could be closed and arranged. It is a sort of Anglo-Catholicism, like the medievalistic theories of Chandler Post, who is a distinguished historian, but they are ideas which can function badly in the brains of North American magnates, distorting their vision of social problems. I guessed it from the conversations X.Y. was having with R. about democracy. It is true of E.R. himself, notwithstanding his Jewish blood: the extent to which he has aspired to certain ideals, and has remodeled himself according to a certain stamp of conservative thinking, is all simply because he has gained entrance almost into the category of public servants through his own function as chief journalist, and because of the "religion" of facts. "Facts" in America have neither profundity nor history; they have no background, so they have a life of their own without needing to be interpreted. On the other hand, men of the Old World know when facts are only apparent and are therefore illusory. In other American circles, those which are the least powerful, there is freedom of spirit: my brother-in-law Perry, for instance, the son of an avid professor of Greek who thought about nothing but Greek, is a very good example. The only abundance which "baronial" families enjoy is the abundance of wealth, and for this wealth there is no objective. We must remember that one century ago the life of the frontier prevailed throughout the whole of America; a life of defense, of society in embryo, of the most primitive provisions for sustenance; and it was from this that the power and influence of this aristocracy developed. The Roman aristocracy in Greece, or in the Latin world itself, met with perfected civilizations which it then helped by giving them the framework of its own organization, and this was the "means," the new wealth, the latest contribution. The objective on which it could act was already formed civilizations, whereas for Americans the objective is empty. A clever young man like X.Y. may start to react, perhaps even violently, against this order of things, but he carries within himself the germs which will make him succumb; he cannot tranquilly, objectively, be "superior," with no reactions, because being that way requires the unconscious deposits of culture which are found in European aristocrats. — Since he is weak, couldn't he be ruined by a woman, by a wife who dominated him? — There is that danger, but I don't believe it is imminent, because although he may not be strong, he is very agile, and nobody will ever possess him; he will always either flee or slip away.

How is it that instead of being strong, sovereign racial types, the scions of these "barons" in general seem fin-de-race, tired, almost degenerate? Because the life that they lead — not their sexual life, but the whole warp and woof of their life — is too febrile and dispersed; in two or three generations they wear themselves out, and this too manifests itself in X.Y.

At the Garden Show the other day, G. was entirely covered with dust from head to toe. Here is a sign that he is a gentleman; only true gentlemen, and true common men, know how to rise above their own appearance; the middle class, with its innumerable subspecies, takes dressing like a mannikin as its ideal. But by now gentlemen are tending to disappear, though not in England.

In England the desire for an unassuming habit has even stranger echoes and manifestations. The old Duke of Northumberland would not condescend to travel in anything but third class. The railroad company of London and North-Eastern was somewhat vexed over this, and when the new branch was put through to Alnwick (his castle) they saw to it that the third class carriages on that line spewed out the poorest of the miners. As soon as he reached the station the Duke saw the invasion, and so what did he do? He bought first class tickets for all the departing miners, and he, alone, went on in third.

I remember that it took me some time to appreciate the beauty of Continental women. During the first months of my sojourn in Paris the French seemed hideous to me. Not the Italians, because it was some time later that I went down into Italy, and furthermore their naturalness made them seem closer to Anglo-Saxon types. If Americans are blind to the beauties in this country, while the young men here are not really blind to American beauties, one must remember that in America the women who are not Anglo-Saxon are the poor women — worn out by household chores and huge families. — Can women's beauty remain beauty even when it touches on vulgarity? — Certainly, and anyone who has been in love often cannot have escaped falling in love with vulgar women.

June 21, 1931

As for that American boy who disappeared during an excursion on Parnassus — it is perfectly clear what happened to him: the dogs devoured him and the shepherds buried him. The Greek government cannot do anything to prevent this danger; it would require an immense police force, even a mobilized army. Greek shepherds, who are Vlach in origin, are the last nomads, and they see foreigners as the symptoms of the civilization which is driving them out and destroying them. Their dogs are like Cerberus — perfectly faithful to their masters, but hostile to the death to anyone who intrudes into their kingdom.

A very important effect of poetry, and of poetic prose, lies in "salivation," in "making your mouth water." If we accept the fact that poetry causes a sensual pleasure, I don't know in what other way it can arouse it. Today Edith Sitwell, with her critique based on p's and b's — the labials and the dentals and their effect in verse — is the first to study the causes of this sensual effect in English poetry, and one can't reproach her for "technicalism" because she gives no absolute rules. Certainly, like anyone who practices an art, she is aroused by the technical problem, and her mind is not particularly adapted to recognizing true, personal poetry — to connecting it with the inspirational sentiment and personality of the artist. But somebody sooner or later had to do what she has done. Many people will heap abuse on her for it, as they shrieked at me when I came out with "tactile values," and now it is I who get angry with them when they see nothing in painting but tactile values! If I had followed my true impulse, instead of losing myself to being a "connoisseur," I would have written tracts on the other arts, following the road on which I began. The arts do not focus uniquely on sight or hearing, which, taken alone, are abstractions, but on complex sensations wherein each sense plays its part. Thus the tactile sense in painting, or the perfume and the taste in words. Even when poetry is read it is always mentally recited, it is always song or refrain; and prose is too; in France it is amazing how much they "sing" in the most ordinary dialogue. English prose can come so close to the richness of poetry that it loses its clarity and perspicuity. The prose of Walter Pater is not a clear crystal which contains his concepts and makes them transparent, but is an ornate and many-colored goblet. Before reaching the juice there is always something to go through, like a complex impediment, the vision of which distracts one from the essence that one would like to attain.

The equality of the Venetian painters does not lie in color itself, even though color is something more than ornamental for them. In the greatest it is always transmuted into beauty of highlights. But in the less great, like Catena, there exists a color which does not shine — I would call it matte — a color which escapes the scintillating, almost glassy appearance of Rubens' work.

I have not yet met any other young Americans like X. — ready as he is to follow any sort of discussion with already "informed" interests; and here at home we talk about everything except problems of high mathematics or theology. But, as for the others, it is not enough; perhaps even he will not be able to resist the "baronial" temptations, the easy position of undisputed authority which he can find in America simply by his being one of the barons.

Paul Cambon was dumfounding in his correctness and in the impersonality of his intellect. When the war broke out, I wanted to return to Italy by car but when I asked him if it were possible he advised me against it. The same evening, when I went home, I found a letter from him which said: "Cher ami, vous m'avez demandé s'il était possible de traverser la France avec votre auto. Je ne puis en aucun cas vous conseiller de le faire: vous vous trouveriez dans un guet-apens de difficultés de toutes sortes. Mais, si vous le faites, je vous engage à montrer autant qu'il vous conviendra cette lettre, pour que les autorités puissent vous venir en aide et vous amoindrir les tracas inévitables en temps de guerre." [1] Perfect diplomatic style: the ambassador freed himself of any responsibility, and yet rendered me the most valid assistance possible. And I only needed to show this letter one single time, upon disembarking.

The best judges of Wilson were the trustees of Princeton University, who considered him intractable and did not wish to hear him spoken of; but they were so vigorously opposed to him that they achieved the reverse effect, and contributed to his enormous popularity. Tyrrell, in London, was the first to tell me that the President would be coming to Paris. I answered that it was unthinkable, impossible, that it would mean the end of any authority he might have. "You'll see," said Tyrrell,[2] so I retorted: "It is you who are making him come." He answered with a smile. Tyrrell knew, as we all did, that it was enough to have Wilson present to make a fool of him, and to reduce his principles, his fourteen points, to zero. I almost had a fit. But the conclusion of peace occurred as it did through the carelessness with which everyone entered the war. One matter which remains unclear is that of the secret treaties: Wilson swore that he had never heard tell

---

[1] "Dear friend, you have asked me if it were possible to cross France with your car. I can under no condition advise you to do it; you would find yourself in a hotbed of difficulties of all sorts. But if you do it, I enjoin you to show this letter whenever convenient so that the authorities may come to your assistance and lessen the inevitable red tape of wartime."

[2] Tyrrell was a high authority in the Foreign Office.

of them; on the other hand Balfour, who was not a liar, guaranteed that he had informed the President about them (of their existence, not their contents). Probably they had been mentioned, but Wilson, all engrossed in the idea of the war, had not taken any notice. His preparation for intervention in European affairs amounted to nothing. With timely negotiations he would have obtained what he wanted because the Allies were in extreme need and the United States was not motivated by personal interest — this fact was of an obviousness which had impressed itself on everyone. In Paris one could not get near him. I remember one day having asked Lippmann if there was any way to do so (Lippmann was on House's staff) and he replied: "Wilson is at the top of a very high tower; there are various platforms around him on which various people stand, according to their political importance, but Wilson does not really have any contact even with them; he is separated from them by a deep chasm." If I wanted to inform Wilson about anything there was only one way to reach him: I would mention it to a woman, a Washington lady in whom he placed greatest confidence and whom he saw any time he needed distraction, though in purest friendship. I had nicknamed her The Eternal Flapper. Little by little, as the months passed, all power was taken from Wilson, and when in certain crises he pulled himself together and threatened to be obstinate and leave, they demonstrated to him that they could do without him and that returning home would only be an embarrassment for him.

Twenty-five or thirty years ago, in Doccia, old Cannon invited me to dinner one evening, and sat me next to Edith

Wharton (who was already famous by then); after ten min-
utes of conversation I felt such an antipathy for her that I
swore in my heart never to see her again. Naturally, whenever I spoke of this encounter I did not hide my sentiments.
Two or three years later, one evening in Paris I received an
invitation to dine at Voisin's; it was early in the summer, so
that when the time came to sit down at the table the lights
were not lit, and there must have been twenty people. They
sat me next to a lady who immediately enchanted me by her
conversation, and when they lit the lights, whom did I see?
Mrs. Wharton. So I told her frankly how amazed I was, and
she confessed to me that that other time she had been so overcome with the desire to know me that her manner must have
been dreadful; even she realized it. This happens to her:
her invincible timidity with new people usually makes her
impossible.

June 22, 1931

In Naples I experienced an ecstasy like that of the Virgin
confronted by the angel of the Annunciation. The miracle is
that civil life in Naples, as in almost all of Italy, should have
endured for three thousand years; in other places this is not
true; there are gaps for centuries. Especially in Greece.

I would like to have the way of the world be that as soon as
one desired a piece of music, players would appear and
would begin to play; the desires would no sooner arise than
they would immediately be satisfied, and yet they would
not produce satiation.

June 23, 1931

I decided to stop seeing Gladys Deacon[1] when I convinced myself that in human relationships she offered nothing but an offensive arbitrariness, pursuing people in a flattering and ensnaring fashion, only so as to be able to break off with them noisily when the fancy struck her. Her last appearance: in 1919 at the entrance of the Petit Palais I saw an old horse-drawn coupé arrive, and out of it step a sort of widow in weeds; I was waiting for other people and was somewhat distracted; how strange, I said to myself, that the Gladys type should be becoming more and more common every day — when suddenly she advanced on me in a fury and almost poked her finger in my eye: "Horrible B.B., you mean you don't recognize me?" Behind her descended, with difficulty, an even more deplorable figure all bundled up in shawls — Boldini.

Salammbô leaves the taste of a thick turtle soup in your mouth.

June 24, 1931

I cannot make up my mind to go back to where the human things of life are listed, classified, botanized, or, worse, proclaimed by concentrated megaphones even to people who do not want to hear. I can no longer tolerate the discussions about art which go on around banquet tables.

[1] A famous American "beauty" of the end of the last century who married the Duke of Marlborough.

No, I will not go to Ireland; I would rather go to China. I will leave it to K.P. to study ninth century crosses and proclaim them superb works of art. The center of my interests lies in classical things; I am one of the few last remaining people who love art in itself, not as archeology, or as paleontology, or as chemistry.

July 5, 1931

When I was a child I remember the pleasure of eating fruit — not what was served at the table; what I loved was any kind of berry I could pull off the trees or pick in the fields. What appealed to me was the act of picking the fruit, of providing for my own needs. Already, by the age of four, the first gestures of independence and autonomous life.

One of D'Annunzio's great defects is that he believes his own lies. To tell lies because they are useful, or through sheer malice, is not a great sin; but to tell lies knowing that they are lies, and then, just because they've been said, to immediately take them for the truth and live accordingly, is a gross sin which falsifies all of life.

Visionaries have no business being in politics. Politics is a trade, and like all trades requires special gifts and training. The politician must clearly see everything that lies around him. We visionaries, on the other hand, are farsighted; what holds our attention in the distance prevents us from seeing what is in the foreground. It is not true, though, that because politics is based on a momentary vision, it should be considered something cheap. Cheap people only go so far as to take part in bureaucracy; he who ascends to the level of politics shows that he is capable of overall vision, but he should not be a visionary and should not even understand them. We want freedom of speech precisely so that the visionaries, who cannot act, may communicate their visions.

I wish that a civilization might be reached in which there were no longer any working hours, but freedom to work; in the sense that everyone might work but everyone would decide on their own when to start and when to leave off, as we do. Thus there would truly be work and leisure. The roughest, most manual labor, that which was most necessary to the community, would be done by recruits. Naturally I am not speaking of the future, I am speaking of a Utopia.

The domination of India keeps the English from acting according to their feelings in politics, from showing what their feelings are. Most of the generals and administrators say "We would like to stop and let India go, but Providence has called on us to govern hundreds of millions of men who without us would be prey to caste wars and civil wars." They say this sincerely, and are not speaking in absurdities. The possession of India is not necessary to English commerce, just as the possession of Argentina isn't, though the English interests in Argentina are enormous. The one thing they feel to be necessary is that India should not be a land of anarchy.

July 6, 1931

In the look of Pienza, as in all things done in the fifteenth century, there is something too minute. The piazza in Pienza really does seem like a stage set, as does the one here at Montepulciano and as does San Biagio, for that matter. There have been two or three times when as I have looked at this view I have seen San Biagio detached from the city, poised on the field, not part of anything. Standing by itself like a model, which could be offered in the palm of one's hand and taken anywhere at all. I am not partial to metaphysical vagaries, but this monument really seems to me to have arisen from some abstract concept, without necessity, without any relation to a purpose — its religious reason being simply a pretext. The whole Renaissance is a phenomenon not so much of the aristocracy as of the intelligentsia, which embraced very few people. Therefore these solitary constructions exist which do not fit together with anything else. I would rather see buildings being like bubbles of water, all at one with a whole mass; I would prefer San Biagio nicely framed as the cathedral of a town. St. Peter's is an example of a church which lives with the world. In the Baroque, contact was made with the earth again — art became popular; and for this reason one can perfectly naturally continue to fabricate Baroque art even today. It is true that country houses — Tuscan farmhouses — follow the sixteenth century type, but the sixteenth century was already a full, hospitable style. What puts me off about the fifteenth century is its strictness, the lack of freedom within those severe lines. Though more graceful, and yet more stingy, that century was still feeling the impact of the Gothic style; the Gothic was its compost.

August 4, 1931

In Americans, even in the best, I see so much futility and so much lack of consciousness that there comes over me a very lively desire to be Swiss instead. And yet the feeling I have for America is almost religious.

What are we, we men, even those among us who are the most interesting — the most richly endowed in culture and in thought? Organ grinders, with a little repertoire of music to "grind," after which we start all over again from the beginning. (Mary: "But I am still at the window listening to you.")

Here is an example of Irish logic: an old lady went to a judge to ask him to grant a divorce to her and her husband. "But why?" asked the judge. "What has happened that at your age you should have such a request? Be patient awhile, the Lord will attend to it." "Ah," answered the old woman, "Your Honor, I suffer the tortures of the damned — I cannot rid myself of doubt as to the birth of my youngest son who is now thirty years old. I am no longer sure that I am his mother."

August 5, 1931

The reputation of *Africa,* Petrarch's Latin poem, is provoked by the difficulty and the boredom of reading it; whoever finishes it is so impressed with the importance of his effort that the few beautiful verses which are to be found in it seem marvelous to him; actually the work has a pallid similarity to the works of Claudian.

Lord Desart (the father of Lady Sibyl[1]) was chattering with Sir Edward Carson one day and said to him: "My dear Carson, I admire you very much, you are a real leader of the masses; I do not share your ideas, but when I follow your political activities I am amazed by your wisdom and your power and the way you are obeyed." "Dear Desart," answered Carson, "yes, I am obeyed and followed in a stupendous fashion; just like the dog of a regiment who frisks around alone in the middle of the road in front of everybody and leads the way for the drummers to march."

Hardtmann, secretary to the Governor of Tunisia, who is a young man full of understanding (half the French who count and who are worth anything have German last names: a sign of France's vitality, that she can totally assimilate whoever falls into her lap) explained to me what the true power in France is, behind the parliament, the government, the press and public opinion: the highest bureaucracy, "les grands commis." There is both good and evil in the power of these people; in part, at least inasmuch as they are "grands banquiers," they are even obeyed by the police, which is not only the instrument but the builder of governments — note the return of Poincaré in 1926, as seen in Halévy's book. The po-

[1] Lady Sibyl Lubbock, mother of the writer Iris Origo.

lice is necessary to power; it is itself the power, and the more a state is centralized, strong, organized, with far-reaching responsibilities, the more the police predominates. The modern state is the police state, even in a free country like England, where, more than an organism for the guarantee of security, it is a great instrument of fiscal power.

Nothing satisfies me the way ancient art does — its necessity, its simplicity, its immediacy, its true humanity, to which I turn as to an essential need. Eating bread, drinking pure water, are the same thing for me.

My memory is like a palimpsest, it no longer has room for even one line of writing.

In my long acquaintance with Montesquiou I never noticed the side for which Charlus is famous: sodomy, and god knows that at that time, young as I was, I made homosexuals' mouths water! We used to pass hours and hours together; I knew he was considered so haughty and difficult, and I was amazed at his desire to speak with me sincerely. One day I said this to him and his answer was: "C'est que vous m'êtes comme un tirage de vingt mille exemplaires." [1] And it was true that I knew how to listen to him. I listened intelligently, not passively, encouraging the conversation along lines which he preferred. Montesquiou was a gentleman, but he was insolent and arrogant: a descendant in spirit of D'Artagnan, who was in fact his ancestor — never vulgar, but

1 "It is that to me you are like a printing of twenty thousand copies."

"voyou" in conduct. In Paris I had no desire to see him; anyone who was close to him became involved, perforce, in his interminable quarrels (herein lay his true resemblance to Charlus). He and Yturri — or Yturri with him — formed a "société d'exploitations" which was utterly devoid of scruples. Yturri was an exile from the Pampas who had set himself up as Montesquiou's publicity manager, the latter thoroughly enjoying the exploitation of any mystification. They milked money wherever they could — at St. Moritz there was pandemonium around a very rich, silly young Italo-Argentine named Bernasconi, who extracted himself noisily out from under their web. I asked Bernasconi if he had ever received pederastic propositions, and he denied it flatly, but everyone was offering this explanation of his relationship with M. Montesquiou's taste was a genuine gift: not the best, perhaps, in certain particulars, but it was his manner of "loving" certain materials, of touching objects, which was like real gold, while in D'Annunzio it became pinchbeck. Montesquiou is the model of Huysman's Des Esseintes,[1] and D'Annunzio is the by-product. Through the book's power of suggestion at first, but then, very quickly, through direct imitation.

The first time I went back to America I had been in Italy seven years and I left my shoes outside the door of my hotel bedroom. But the following morning I found them still dirty, so I rang for the bellboy who explained to me that I would find a place to have them shined on the main floor. Sure enough no sooner had I gone down than I found myself in the hands

[1] In his novel *À Rebours*.

of a perfect shoeshine boy who spoke English with a strong Italian accent; I started to speak to him in Italian and he said, "Oh, now I see — you are the Florentine tenor." To that Neapolitan, my accent was utterly Florentine, and in that hotel the only Italians who could ever come were tenors.

Why is it that liberalism, or any other "party," current idea, or form of thought all of a sudden ceases to have any "worth" or to set firmly, so that once again the absolutists take over, with the opposite form of thought? It is because the problems are never "resolved," but are set aside at a certain point, and public interest is then attracted by others which are more carefully considered and evaluated according to some opposite criterion, an opposite way of thinking, opposite principles. Are the liberals in power, or do they dominate public opinion? There will come a day when people will be tired of hearing the same things repeated and the same arguments gone over; forgotten problems will rise to the surface — problems which the conservatives, the absolutists, were used to discussing and from which the people became separated for no real reason. Thus it is possible for "returns"; things can be taken up again from the uncertain and inconclusive point where they were left. But, vice versa, against this possibility stands the fact that any thought, truly thought out, will not have been thought in vain; in some way it endures and counts for the future.

August 7, 1931

Time, not objective Time which I do not bother about, but subjective Time, is symbolized for me by an accordion. To me, far and near are interchangeable terms when applied to Time. When I was studying, Athens became the only fact of the day for me; Time (and Space) was reduced to zero by the passion with which I relived and came to know the ancient world. Athens was closer to me than Boston. And this happens for anyone who has a concrete imagination.

This idea of the elasticity of Time is found in Shakespeare's *As You Like It,* presented by the clown, in whom the seeds of so many other ideas and problems in the plays are found. Thus the reading of Shakespeare, which is very easy insofar as it is adventurous and dramatic storytelling (at the age of twelve I was reading it fluently) becomes difficult when one acquires consciousness of how much is contained in it. The difficulty is augmented by incorrect texts and the careless writing — the fever with which Shakespeare wrote, patching together old things, possessed by the demands of the stage to produce for the stage, and quite indifferent to any orderly exposition which reading his dramas would necessitate.

Being more easily accustomed to solitude, it is natural that women, little as they may have the disposition for it, conceive a passion for abstract thinking, for formulating everything in concepts; and in fact one does find a predisposition for "concept" in many women; but philosophical women, no. Something intervenes which hinders their minds from following the road right to the end.

Naples, the city of abstract thought. Perhaps also because thought, let us say pure thought, is associated with a certain laziness, a dreaminess, an insouciance about precise, prosaic multiplicities of facts.

In New York, for all that one does there, or thinks one is doing, the way of life is colonial; there is a desperate ambition to imitate everything that is done in London, in greater bulk.

I knew Barrès. I spoke to him once for a couple of hours. I found him closed and obscure. A curious look about him — like a gypsy, great timidity, and impossibility for self-expression. Interested in asking me for opinions and news, but about Chinese art; which means that he had been informed adequately as to my capabilities, not restricting them to the Florentine school. But he understood and cared little about art, and in fact it only enters his books by historical association, and his emotion is all directed at nature.

Even for me reading is a springboard, but I do not take the leap from the book to "the abstract quintessence" — I stop halfway. Since my youth I have, yes, "quintessencized." Now it is history books which attract me, those which give me reasons for things and whose ideas arise from facts, not historical narratives. A great historian: Eduard Meyer. He examines sources critically, and once the sources are reconstructed the sequel of facts is rendered plausible.

By the completion of my seventh year I no longer believed that I was the center of the universe, and since then, one might say, I have never changed. I have never again been able to detach myself from the thought of others, except perhaps in rare moments of ecstasy. Education should do this: take from us the idea that we are co-extended with the universe, which is a child's idea.

August 8, 1931

English conversation is not difficult either for its structural logic or for its vocabulary; but for the continual recurrence of metaphor, phrases and even single words taken from the poets, the significance of which only carries weight through the remembrance of a verse, of a stanza, or of a poem: golden words in the most simple conversation, like the golden threads woven into fifteenth century tapestries.

Philosophers, all of them, adopt words which recur continually without their having defined them; each has his favorite; for instance the word "spirito" for Croce. I understand more or less what he means but I would like him to explain it himself. They are like clothespins, or like a bus which carries everything and everybody. I prefer the one-seat carriage.

Then there are those (philosophers) who trail behind. Gentile went in a sidecar; the sidecar was wrecked and he was left to go on foot.

I like Sargent's earlier paintings; I dislike his women, and even more his well-preserved men in their military uniforms, or hunting costume. An anecdotal and psychological painter; not really "historical" in the sense of "revealing" history, unless the history he reveals is Loliée's history. For this reason little of him will remain. It will remain better in photographs of the paintings than in the paintings themselves; the colors fade and are not beautiful. He has cultivated and rendered an impudently elegant appearance in the women; and one can understand the anecdote which occurred in Boston during a lavish exposition of his works. A friend of mine, Ross, was circulating around the room and was snorting to himself; another man came up to him and asked him what he was muttering between his teeth: "I am repeating to myself the title of one of Wordsworth's poems: 'Intimations of Immorality!' "

Like all the most honest and aware painters, Sargent only admired the painting of artists whose principles agreed with his, and who threw light on his own work: El Greco and Tiepolo — and he was one of the recent promoters of their reputation.

Péguy speaks of the religious sense with which he entered the Louvre for the first time, and of how he could not tear himself away from the pictures. My first experience, when I arrived in Paris on my twenty-second birthday, was the same. I had been prepared by an American education, which was faithful to tradition; I was predisposed to admire the whole past which they had told me about at Harvard. And the feeling which accompanied me in my visits to the galleries was absolutely one of religious awe, a religious and reverential terror. Not that I lacked understanding — my direction was solid — for while I didn't "disadmire" anything, my admiration was certainly justifiable, and I cannot say that I have reformulated my judgments since then. On the other hand I was modest, and therefore I did not proclaim them rigidly, and in discussions I tried to respect the current authoritative opinions and to persuade myself of them, holding my own doubts in reserve. I had a mystical attitude toward art, and I still realize that the aesthetic experience is mystical, a mysticism which has no need to believe in objectivity, in the reality of the object, and which is thus a pure mysticism. As happens for all mystics, there came that dry time when everything seemed to turn to ashes, so I retreated a bit, turning it all over in my mind, trying out theories in which I did not believe, and it was then that I met Mary. Mystics know hours of darkness and of abandonment, and unless they override them, they fall. It came (this dryness) from the rationalizing impulse which accompanied my most intense sensations; it made me want to "explain to myself" my "feeling" for art, and to give myself some reason for it; so long as I felt something and had not reflected about it, it was a torment. Then one day, in front of San Pietro in Spoleto, I understood: suddenly a clear idea both of art and of the word — the formula which could express it — were revealed to me together. I recognized the vital value of art, of art consisting in "vitality," its function as being "life enhancing," the exalter of life. From then on I was at the center of the problem, I could work; I have never left off since, and I have not changed. More and more clearly I have understood what I

wanted to do in setting out to write. Writing has this importance, that it renders ideas clearly, it orders them in words,
in propositions. Until they are written, formulated, they cannot even be considered properly thought out.

The history I would like is a history of civilization, not a
history of facts nor of institutions. Art was the organizer of
civilization; it is art which enriches and "produces" us; this is
something I would like to investigate. Works of art are "evidence"; one may have intuitions, glimmerings, but one does
not trust one's own ideas nor have the courage to proclaim
them, unless an existing work of art provides us with a prece-
dent. The impressionists — the true ones, Monet and Sisley,
for example — did not leave "great" or many works of art,
but they "saw" nature in a new way and enabled others to
"see it" in that way. Since their work we can speak of red or
purple or violet shadow; before them shadows were always
black. Thus we see the landscape according to an artistic
education which by now may be unconscious, but which is
nonetheless real. And, to continue this further, the word explains and "educates" feeling. Previous to the word one cannot say that even the most elementary of relationships —
that between a man and a woman — really exists.

It has been my dream and my hope to "prepare" work for
my disciples and to prepare my disciples for the work which
I desire and foresee. It doesn't finally matter whether or not
they derive unsuspected or contrary results from the premises which I propose. I wish them well along their own roads,

so long as they depart from a clearly envisioned rationale and in good conscience. The bad thing is that the young are not so anxious to be in accord with their elders as with their contemporaries, with the clamor all around them, and they simply add more of the identical, ephemeral clamor.

Artists should not "believe" in the things they have produced, but in the things which they will produce, in the humanity which remains in them, not in that which is already expressed and siphoned off in their works. For this reason I am uncomfortable when people speak to me of my work, even if I realize that they are speaking sincerely. Only people who are born fatuous, or everyone perhaps in their fatuous moments, are proud of their own work. Unfortunately among painters and sculptors fatuousness reigns supreme; with very few of them, with none, perhaps, except Matisse, can I discuss anything. Besides fatuousness there is a predominance in them of a romantic formula and training which makes them feel gigantic and use enormous words. Whistler's arrogance was an example of this, and all of them retain something of a similar arrogance.

I don't want people to have too clear or definite opinions, in which no surprise awaits me. I already know all the neat opinions, so in France, where everyone values clarity above all things, I feel as though I were in a desert. Instead I like to be the midwife of confused and painful opinions which are struggling to reach the light of day and in which one feels some effort and pains. Like Lessing: between the two offer-

ings of God: the sack of truth on the one hand and that of
the search for truth on the other, I opt for the second.

(Addressed to Clotilde Marghieri): Clotilde, you must let
your hair grow and then you will look absolutely like an
Ingres or a Chassériau. A Chassériau. A Chassériau most
of all. You don't know who he was? He was Ingres' best disciple. He could have held Puvis de Chavannes' post, and done
it very much greater honor, but Puvis knew this, detested
him, and did everything possible to obliterate not only his
memory but even his work. The mural paintings of the Cour
des Comptes are said to have survived in great part, after the
fire of 1871 during the time of the Paris Commune, and, had
they been transported, could have been saved; but Puvis saw
to it that they be destroyed.

The Contesse de Noailles, the poetess, had become the idol
of Parisian society, as Valéry was later. Paris is so skeptic, as
a city, that it always needs to make itself "gobeuse."

August 10, 1931
My friend C.M. has a mind which moves on a vertical line,
from the bottom to the top, toward the zenith. I have known
many like her. They have no need of information; culture
does not interest them, but as they read or question, what
they want are resting points and jumping-off points — spring-
boards from which to launch themselves.

I don't think German loyalty is praiseworthy; I have not
experimented with German friendships, nor do I warrant

that the cultural world is exempt from vulgar interests and baseness; quite the contrary: I know that it is a center of unimaginable dishonesty and professional corruption. But nonetheless there also exist in Germany phenomena of a submission which is almost feudal — of men who put themselves in "liege" to another man, to an idea, or a system — phenomena which stem more from dullness of character than from disinterested, healthy enthusiasm, and this by contrast with other nations — France for example.

Mary frightens me when she says she is well; she says it and feels it with such exaltation that one senses that she may be on the verge of some misfortune. It is the hubris of the Greeks; it is that insolent condition which used to attract the vengeance of the gods. The same is true of America: America does not want grief, it does not want tragedy, it does not want to think about either one or the other. This is a condition of spirit which strikes terror in my heart; it is the contrary of civilization. Despite all the means at an American's disposal, he is cut off from the world in a way which not even a Calabrian peasant is. The latter, though almost mute, understands and lives the reality which surrounds him. The American does not understand. He does not understand the catastrophe of the *Titanic*,[1] he does not understand the meaning and the possibility of a calamity of that sort, or how it could ever happen. The Americans were stunned by it to no effect.

[1] The transatlantic liner which hit an iceberg and sank, in 1914.

The English, on the other hand, cope with life in this way: one can know little of the reality of the external and internal world, or of human destinies, but "one knows" that there are the rules: the rules of tennis, the rules of golf, the rules of life, and it is to these that one must cling. Thus they promote a way of life which is very favorable to freedom and to responsibility: a comfortable, decorous system which they term "fair play." Certainly they too minimize the "tragic sense" of life; it does not enter the game. But, as opposed to the Americans, they are not terrified by it; and jolts occur frequently among the English — sudden immersions into tragedy, into drama, into the sublime. Their literature gives so many examples of it: from Shakespeare to *Wuthering Heights,* the poets, the (tragic) humorists. Their life, being so well ordered, and ordered in a muted register, facilitates their freedom of vision and of the artistic sense. Think of the English novelists who are never moralists; who simply narrate, and in so doing bring their characters to life without "problems." While among the French there will always be morality; the "casuistry" surrounding situations, or surrounding any "idea" whatever that the author may hold as pre-existent and conclusive.

What do we want, we liberals? Not that there be no authority in the state, but that its justification be moral rather than by force, and therefore that it be more securely founded on general consent. Not much police, and in general not many "authorities," because the "authorities" become autonomous organisms, and the more powerful they are the more they place the state in danger, giving rise to a pretorian conscience in their leaders and in the more adept among them.

I call Chinese paintings — the great scrolls — synopses, as one says symphony; they are pure landscape, not ordered, condensed landscape. The figures only exist in them — very tiny — to give the proportions.

August 11, 1931

A great deal of diplomacy is necessary for success in the university world; the famous professors are great politicians, great administrators of their own activities and of their own success.

The exercise of criticism does not leave any trace in literature. We pass through, we have a minute of importance, and then we disappear. Who in Italy today remembers Nencioni, or, in France, Emile Montégut, Philarète Chasles, Saint Victor, Jean-Jacques Ampère? In England the names of a few critics have survived because of the beautiful prose they have written, not because of the importance of their work.

"Archeological" professors cease to understand anything when it comes to recent works; "inspired" poets don't know anything when they are faced with passing judgment on a work. D'Annunzio could bring himself to write as sublime a page on a painting recommended by Baedeker with three stars as on the last piece of current trash on which his eyes

happened to fall. Open the tap and the water ran, quite ir-
respective of the value.

Faces are like rivers; it is always the same water which
flows, the only difference lies in the banks (the cut and coif-
fure of the hair).

Whether I am working or idle, time always passes very
swiftly for me. Only in traveling do I stretch it out, multiplying, as it were, Time by Space. And who knows whether
or not, through the modern theories which make a single essence of Time and Space, there may be an objective reality
behind this subjective interpretation.

Everyone has heard the story of Bettino Ricasoli, who,
learning of his wife's love for a Petrovic (relative of the rulers
of Montenegro) took the main gate of the palace off its
hinges one day so that when the lover entered it fell on him
and crushed him with its weight; the wife was then relegated
to Brolio.[1] It is such a well-known story that Ricasoli's biog-
raphers feel obliged to excuse it.

Ellen Terry, who was married to and living with Craig
(Gordon's father), walked out on him one day for no reason.
Craig was very very unhappy about it. He fell sick and im-
plored so bitterly that finally he did obtain his wife's return.
After a little while, when he saw her, he begged: "Let me see
the children." "It is impossible," replied Ellen. "But why?"
"My dear, it is utterly impossible; I told them you were dead

[1] A medieval castle near Sierra.

and have been taking them every day to weep on your tomb." The same Ellen Terry was the wife of Watts for a brief time. She got fed up, and one day when they had invited guests she came down to dinner completely nude, just to create a scandal. And this at a time (sixty years ago, that is!) when in America, which is to say in the most provincial of the English provinces, the resentment in the face of "nudity" was such that the following could have happened to me (and this would have been twenty years later): I was a student at Harvard and my room was on the top floor of a building that looked out over an open park; no house in front for a considerable distance. In the winter, with the windows closed, as soon as I woke up I never hesitated to do my gymnastic exercises nude, in front of the window, because I could see better. A classmate from the nearest house across the way managed to see me, and he came over to tell me that if I did not stop he would have to report me to the University proctors.

August 12, 1931

The "Ode to Autumn" is perhaps to me the most beautiful poem in the world; each word is filled with an "autumnal" sense, yet the result is not too rich because they are all serving one and the same end. It is a marvelous example of what I call "significant detail."

Can one say that Chinese civilization is provincial? Yes, if one means, by provincial, autonomous; and by the same token occidental civilization seems provincial to the Chinese.

Autonomous it certainly is; its communication with the Indo-European world, through Buddhism, is as tenuous as the thread of sand which passes through the neck of an hourglass. Provincial, in any case, applies to the Parisian for whom only Paris counts in all the world, or to the Berliner infatuated only by Berlin. — But in Paris people's minds are open to all foreign and universal things? — No, only to universal bons mots.

You needn't see the ocean to know that there is salt.

Death never comes at an opportune time; if it did, there would be no murders.

August 13, 1931
Reading verses metronomically (as Robert Trevelyan does) is the fruit of an anti-romantic prejudice. They should be read so that the cadence and the rhythm assist the sense. Every art must be interpreted humanistically; if not it becomes reduced to technique.

1900 by Morand: a work by a traveling salesman of lingerie for "cocottes."

Reading new things with the sole purpose of "being au courant" is one of the sins against the spirit. Not more than a tenth of one's time and a tiny part of one's energy (which is always less than one expects) should be dedicated to new things. What is this "current"? It is a tiny, almost subterranean rivulet which appears in a few salons; and meanwhile there are currents, or rather there is one current, which is truer than the one you think of in referring to fashion. The newspapers, yes, one reads for the "news" which they announce; but it is reading which involves very little strain, especially for someone who, like myself, is used to five thousand years' worth of written chronicles. — Does reading new works help exercise critical taste? — This is a misguided notion. Taste is exercised by innocently re-experimenting with what is beautiful on its own account in works already admired. It cannot be exercised freely in new things; too much of our personal future enters into anything which is in the formative stages — our desires and doubts, hopes and fears. Interests converge which are not aesthetic, from which we cannot separate ourselves. If we are honest, and clear-sighted, we have to admit that there is no comment one can make on the new products of the day. Likewise one can never be sure of the "duration" of the work of art, except at a definite and fairly considerable distance, because this duration is measured by the permanence of our interests and our vision of things; in a word, of our civilization. Let us take two centuries as a yardstick; let us go back, that is, to the publication of *Robinson Crusoe;* don't we perhaps read it in the same spirit with which we read, let's say, a novel written fifty years ago? But at that time there appeared many writings of the same type, constructed almost the same, that we would read today with almost equal pleasure; yet that one alone has stood out. — And two hundred years from now? — The path of the future is more arduous, because today, with the expansion of publication, technical "methods" have grown and are widespread, so many psychical and ethical and aesthetical "gimmicks" have been invented and taught — in a word, the "level" is so much higher. And what do we deduce from it? That the struggle to conquer (Time) will be harder than ever; that only a minimal percentage of the works which are produced will emerge.

Turning one's gaze to the past, we cannot feel sure of the fame of a poet like Baudelaire; if we were honest we would see that we are too optimistic in the tone of our own appreciation. We can be sure of the great English and Italian poets of the beginning of the nineteenth century; of the Russian novelists up to and including Chekhov; and I would say of Proust, if you reduce the work to *Swann's Way* and perhaps a third of all the rest. But the work which Time respects is never a corpus, it is always a selection. We cannot be sure of D'Annunzio (perhaps two verses will remain) or Conrad, who writes adolescent stories, or Ibsen. At times Ibsen touches on "eternal," not merely social problems, but how does he treat them? Does he treat them in an eternal manner?

Those who believe in the current, the "innovators," those who swear by the word of today, esteem new works and delight in new worlds and in new orders as in a revelation, to contrast with all the past. But the truth is that one cannot add anything to the already rich humus of our culture except a delicate superficial stratum of mold; a stratum which, from contact with the old, will then become fertile, and indistinguishable as humus.

Using another of my favorite images I can say that people count who add a brick to this House of Life where we live, keeping as we do our awareness of a civilization which is not purely material. There are many people in this house, and some argue and make a racket, but whoever puts on a new brick of his own is he who offers the greatest contribution and whose name endures.

About the "current," there is a thought of Nietzsche's which goes somewhat as follows: if you want to be distinguished from the crowd it can be for two reasons; either because it disgusts you or because you want to put yourself at its head. This second motivation has never been mine; I have always remembered that the first in a flock is still always a sheep.

One can philosophize at the age of twenty, when one reveals oneself and breaks out with one's own lyrical effusions. Afterwards, in protracting them and living them, philosophical ideas become a prison throughout one's entire life.

August 14, 1931

The greatness and the novelty of Milton lies in his having been the first to feel our modern universe as infinite. For Dante the universe was all compact, in sections — a larger house in which this little house, the Earth, could be found embedded.

"Nice people? Boronia is full of nice people."

August 15, 1931

Emerson is not an artist when he is writing poetry; he did not study either rhythm or rhyme, so his rhyme and rhythm have something crude and rough about them — a sort of rustic beauty. But even in the poetry he reveals his major gift, which is the capacity for direct contact with reality without intermediate screens. Almost all of us interpose garish curtains between ourselves and reality — sometimes many-colored and perfumed curtains; immediate communication is a province of the very few — that open contact like the touch of a clapper on a bell. In Emerson, no matter what he is dealing with, one always feels it. His failing stems from the people among whom he was born and lived; he is inbred in the hard, uncultivated Puritanism of the New World; if he had been born elsewhere he would have emerged as a genius — in Frankfurt he would have been a Goethe. He is therefore both better and worse than his English contemporaries, who lived in an entirely different atmosphere. One should remember that Puritanism in America reached the point of considering all products of the intellect as inimical, something which never occurred in England. Carlyle, that master of the English conscience, is an immoralist who took himself seriously and whom the public has considered to be moral. Carlyle is infatuated by childish admiration for any willful or capricious acts, and exalts beyond the limits of possibility some of the most twisted or paltry figures, because he seemed to see in them this power which prostrated him. (His depiction of Francha, the ephemeral dictator of Montevideo, is typical.) Wordsworth comes closer to Emerson for a puritanical constitution, but how much more fortunate he was with respect to the culture and the psychic climate in which he lived! Even closer, without, however, reaching the point of rebellion, are the descendants of that age, the new Bloomsbury rebels: Quakers and descendants of Quakers, issuing from their own shells with great difficulty — Roger Fry and Clive Bell and the Stracheys, and even Virginia Woolf.

Who is not in history? Even Heliogabalus and Nero are in it. Actually history is strewn with horrible and futile acts.

There are human relationships which make one think of an hourglass; one single extreme point of contact, a point through which barely a thread passes. Often sexual relationships are like this: take away that point and there is nothing else, nothing human, in common.

August 16, 1931

The work of Maurice Baring is like a "débit d'eau sucrée." The vogue for Baring stems from the fact that he belongs to the best English society and yet has deigned to become Catholic; thus he satisfies the refined materialism of the "Ritzonians." [1] When he returned from Russia it was the moment in which for some recondite reason (perhaps the secret instigation of the Foreign Office) Russia became fashionable.

So Baring took it upon himself to commit rash actions — to

[1] Berenson's neologism for the frequenters of Ritz Hotels — i.e., the café society of the time.

pull hair and wigs and necklaces off ladies and to throw
everything into the fire or out of the window. Thus he became irresistible, and since that time his fame has not dwin-
dled.

Dante Gabriel Rossetti: poet of enchantment, a tapestry
whose threads are words.

Death in Venice, by Thomas Mann is a sad and rather
putrid work, precisely because it is trying to represent a refined and perfumed state of the soul; odor of "patchouli," a
complex odor based on oil which has gone bad. Like anything German which tries to be elegant, it comes out as extremely rustic and inept. Schiller's Venice (he never went
there) is much more alive. Romantic, yes, but belonging to
that first, noble Romanticism, not to that final Romanticism
which tended toward the lurid and swampy. Why waste
time reading a book of this sort? I read (novels) either because I am attracted by the vividness of the narrative, by
the roller coaster of the tale (W. Scott, Dumas, Manzoni) or
because the characters are plausibly presented to me, and are
not just plausible but necessary — in a certain sense typical,
allegorical. It is stated again and again that the German professor in *Death in Venice* is a professor, but he isn't really;
the Polish family is a family of tremendous "rasta" but they
are not seen as "rastas," they are taken as being pure gold.

What is the significance of English silence, and to what
does it correspond? Certain circles specifically create the
cult of "disposition," proclaiming the rule which forbids do-

ing anything to which one is not "disposed," so when you don't feel like talking you don't talk. Ray Strachey and her husband Oliver (who ate lunch with me one day reading the *Times*) are initiates of this cult, as are Arthur Waley and Percy Lubbock. Not Lytton Strachey; his is a more complex case. He has painted himself a "lid" — a false, hieratic, strident configuration of himself, like the lids which cover mummies, which are enlarged, mechanical repetitions of their features and behind which they hide. It is not his true being, but only that "lid" of his, which he presents to whoever is speaking with him.

The chestnut trees with their bark all worked over with lines and nerves; an effect exactly like that of the most perpendicular Gothic — of the choir in Westminster Abbey.

Today the light is confusing the planes of the distance into one — flat and vague; it is like the substance of an old watery piece of glass, with no more transparency left.

August 17, 1931

I foresee a day when cities, and even the country, will be dissolved and everything will be an indistinguishable suburb, as the Riviera is today from Marseilles to Naples. Industries will multiply even in Italy, when the costs of energy become so low that it can reach any place without too much difficulty, and agricultural Italy will be transformed into garden culture, enclosed in little rectangles behind each house. Does this mean a prediction of widespread wealth? Certainly, and wealth which will descend to a level of worse than mediocre convenience — made manifest by the most squalid type of "cottage" construction possible. One already sees signs of it on the Italian beaches, transformed as they are into the most trite suburbs — not even into "de luxe" suburbs as beaches are elsewhere. I predict an age of a deformed and vulgar aesthetic; I do not, however, predict the death of beautiful buildings, because I believe that men have an inextinguishable thirst for beauty and that they can extract it from any new and necessary forms whatever, when they are accustomed to them. Furthermore, industry based on electrical energy changes the equipment of buildings so that they are no longer that type of smokestack factory with deposits of coal next to piles of debris which have been so offensive to us. And in Italy particularly; because here, wherever people have been aware of modern necessities, nobody has shown any reserve or hesitation. Factories and products were constructed to be as massive and violent in aspect as possible, perhaps in reaction to the abundance of "lovely things" around them. Right down to details: I remember how offensive the first fixtures for electric light were — nothing more than pears hanging from the ceiling, or "arms" stuck onto the walls. Already in 1887 before I left Boston they had the idea there of illuminating houses deceptively — of giving artistic shapes to the lights, which instead of being meager and mechanical became perhaps even too artistic and ornamental.

There is something in America's physical configuration which prevents the extension of civilization. The geological formation of New England is one of the most ancient. Buried basalt attests to the possibility of human habitation in that region prior to that of the most archaic regions of the old world, and yet, when they discovered it, they found that man had almost disappeared from there without leaving any vestige of a durable civilization. Explanation of this phenomenon can be found in the terrible climate. In the old Eurasian continents the mountain chains go from east to west, and thereby "shelter" the regions which they separate: sheltering them respectively from great cold and great heat. The system of longitudinal chains which exists in North America leaves the habitable zones at the mercy of the most fierce changes of temperature, from the frosts which descend all the way to Virginia, to the heat which rises all the way to Canada. It is the opposite of a temperate climate. The result is that the air is extremely stimulating, but also harmful.

Psychically, the influence of the climate combining with the scarcity of original civilization means that what triumphs is a desire for seizing the moment, and for novelty, accompanied by precocious, extremely rapid decadence and inadequate physical resistance. And the generations do not endure. What little freshness and vitality one can unearth in the American people is owed to the proximity in which any refined and intellectual person of the New World finds himself with the peasants of the Old — the rapid transition, in two generations, from the spade and the shepherd's crook to the "baronial" condition. But already there is a dearth of descendants among the American barons of today, as is apt to happen in any metropolis. A third generation of "Pari-

sians" does not exist; nuclei of "cockney" remain in the cities
(the way in America the "stock" perpetuates itself in the
"poor white" or "white trash," living quite cut off from the
main stream), but these people maintain conditions of life
which are both archaic and secret; they do not either count
or have any part in the life of the city.

Julius Caesar was a mixture of Carlo di Rudinì[1] and Mussolini.

August 18, 1931

Morra, working with his pincers the way one does to pull
the last little piece of meat from the claw of a lobster, has by
now extracted from us all the information possible about our
entire life, and must now know it down to the least detail, as
we know it ourselves.

No, X. cannot have any acquaintance with what counted
for me at Oxford — with what, I dare say, is the best of Oxford: the intellectual tradition of philosophical, metaphysical thought, which is produced almost "globally," without
light from any great stars, by reason of the mutuality of life
and purpose of worthy, sincere men, who breathe the same
air, saturated with culture. The rest of Oxford is a matter of
fashion; it is not important at all.

I only came to know Proust during the war: dirty, untidy,
with a voice like a peacock — a bad imitation of Montes-

---

[1] The Marquis Carlo Starabba di Rudinì, son of the Sicilian statesman,
typical D'Annunzio high society figure, ended in suicide.

quiou. His conversations were like his letters, interminable explanations of why he could not stay longer, or could not be seen more often (walking back and forth in Place Vendôme). He was eaten alive by snobbery. Montesquiou was his ideal: the man who was related to all the French nobility and who, to let off steam, could fly into a rage and break with everyone, insult everyone, let loose the tidal wave of his impetuousness without paying heed to anything (Montesquiou would not allow anyone to take a snapshot of him an instant before he had assumed an appropriate attitude, but in spite of this all his "gestures" in life were absolutely spontaneous). Proust admired his "crânerie," but in trying to imitate him resulted in a sort of abjection. (He was never at his ease, for example, but he wanted to appear free and easy, making a great show of aplomb which was entirely secondhand.)

Gladys Deacon was like Trilby, that beautiful and divine singer who did not know a note, ended up tone-deaf, and could do nothing without her prompter. Principal prompters for Gladys: Montesquiou and myself. She did not really know how to "learn" but she could retain everything which would be useful to her in making an effect. Her "effects" have since ended in almost complete solitude; by now all people have deserted her, and nothing remains of her but a myth. She was, in former days, like Venus' cat — that cat who was made into a beautiful woman by the grace of the goddess, but could not remain in the company of women because she would suddenly spring and devour any little mouse that appeared. Gladys Deacon's "mouse" was a need to dominate, to crush under her heel the heads of those who were weaker than she. Thus no sooner would she see a possible victim than she forgot everything else, even her deepest interests, and would set out to pursue him until she had led him to his end. This is what ruined her.

October 31, 1931
   Scarfoglio's[1] feeling for women? The virility of Scarfoglio? It is not a question of any of this. Between Scarfoglio and women there did not exist a physiological rapport, but a tropism, a chemical reaction, which was precise and inevitable.

   Just what is the "personality" of an individual and where is it hidden? I see that now several of my illustrious American colleagues feel justified in denying many of Signorelli's drawings because they are not "personal" enough, because they do not have the sublime and exclusive quality of others which are his best. I too am studying him again, and I am convinced that you cannot limit his activity to those works which seem most clearly "personal," but that in the work of an artist who lived almost eighty years there can be even four or five veins of different "personalities." But which will be the true, fundamental one? There are the drawings done with a sureness, great steadiness and a richness which place them on a par with those of Michelangelo; but then there are many others which, though contemporary with the first, are softer and more uncertain in their execu-

   1 Carlo Scarfoglio, living Italian journalist and writer.

tion, such as the studies for the Orvieto frescoes. If the real Signorelli were the Michelangelesque one, how did it happen that he could sink to the level of the other draftsman? It is my opinion that the "personal" Signorelli is the "mou et flou" one; but that when he was favorably disposed and found a stimulus in works which he admired by the greater artists, he was able to surpass himself and emulate them, so that certain qualities which seem absolutely his are not really talents of his elementary "personality" but represent conquests of his will and application. It is this energetic effort, not the qualities it achieves, which is the salient point of his nature. I apply these observations to myself and I ask myself every moment if my capacity for concentration is intense enough — enough to produce the maximum results of which I am capable; the answer is never reassuring. If work were the simple result of "personality" I would have no doubt. If only all the force which I waste in living with all my senses open could be concentrated on one point, while I remained dumb to the rest! Meanwhile time has gone by, and I must discard problems (innumerable visions which present themselves to me) which are outside the scope of my closed road.

November 1, 1931

Mrs. Wharton: I like F., but I really don't know what one can talk to him about.

B.B.: There is no need to talk to him; he is like a good faithful dog who is occasionally surly.

Mrs. Wharton: But B.B., I can talk to a dog for hours at a time.

B.B.: All right, all the better; do the same thing. Speak to him as you would speak to a dog and you'll see that there will be no lack of conversation.

November 2, 1931

Here in Italy one never sees unfinished faces, attempts at faces, such as those which populate the pages of the *Illustrated London News* and *Town and Country*, where there are portraits of all the illustrative couples on their wedding days; faces, as the boy in Sacchetti's story says, like those of the Baronzi — the oldest Florentine family, which grew up before God had learned to draw. It is an observation which I can only imagine coming from two mouths: a fifth century Greek and a Florentine of that time.

The same prejudice — a generic boredom and contempt — bothers me about both Browning and Wagner, and it vanishes in the same way, when the particular "piece" is in front of me and its beauty conquers me once again.

San Martino alla Palma[1] is the rustic Parthenon.

Vernon Lee thinks that I have a little secret key and that all I need to do is take it out of my pocket for her to see it and make use of it; a little key which, once possessed, would explain the mystery of all things. If only I were a little bit gen-

1 A Renaissance country church in the outskirts of Florence.

erous, just once! I would let her hold it in her hand, after which she would never have to ask me anything again. When I first knew her, she ascertains, I was only interested in Arabic poetry. Actually the story goes as follows: I was in Florence for the first time — very young (very handsome, according to her, and I am convinced; also very seductive, but this I have no way of knowing) and I had a letter for her which she told me to deliver at her house at about ten o'clock some evening when I had nothing else to do. I went one evening and found a flock of women around her (she was uglier than she is today) all striking more or less Botticellian poses, all breathing an aura of acute Renaissance. What was I going to do in the midst of them? I had to interest them and stupefy them with something which they would never have thought of. I knew a little bit about Arab poetry, and I spoke about Arab poetry, and I brought her a volume of translations which furthermore I didn't believe she would ever give back. I heard no more about Vernon until she appeared one day in the Bergamo Gallery, or rather I appeared to her, completely absorbed in taking notes without even recognizing her. Which is how she came to know me as an art critic.

November 10, 1931

Corot and Degas repeat the characteristics of the Florentine painters, especially Degas. His paintings are Pollaiuolo drawings. Corot's landscapes in his "Italian period" are not reminiscent of Fra Bartolomeo; he was a lyricist of nature, whereas Corot constructs it, is its architect, its "carpenter," as Michelangelo was with the human body. When Michelangelo is not being rhetorical, when he has his material well under his hands and is enthusiastic about it, he is the artist who better than any other points toward the possibilities which blossomed in the art of the last century. A Michelangelo horse only finds its equal in a horse by Degas; this I have already written in my book on drawings. Yes, it was in my youth that I accepted the exile of staying here in Florence, and now I have become as accustomed to it as though it were my true home. It was an exile into which I moved from Paris, where my impulse had been to study the art of the nineteenth century.

As soon as Conrad touches land, or as soon as he comes into a port, he has the capacity with few figures and with just a little foreshortening to single out in a marvelous way the characteristics most particular to the country where he has arrived. His brief story "Il Conde" is a typical example, wherein in the sketch of one character, and in one moment of one character, Naples appears in its entirety. Gobineau was able to achieve the same thing even better than Conrad, though through other means.

The "character of a people" is not something to take seriously from a scientific point of view, but it is an abstraction to which one always returns in any discussion; it is the impression which is obtained by taking the characteristics common to any nation, as a whole, over and above the fundamental human characteristics.

February 6, 1932

In his latest play O'Neill transplants Cassandra into the time of the Civil War, against an American background — an attempt which seems to me to be illegitimate — even immoral. Every age, every country, must find its artistic inspiration in what pertains to it. It was Rome which set a bad example. With their nouveau riche psychology the Romans fully appreciated the benefits which could be furnished by a civilization which had reached its peak, and did not set out to remodel them on their own account. But what does America have to do with Greece? America is the just inheritor of the Anglo-Saxon legacies, and of them it can avail itself. This pose of remaking the classics, transferring them to the atmosphere of today, is a Latest Fashion, originating in France; Cocteau, Gide, and finally Joyce's *Ulysses*. But whoever really amounts to anything finds his inspiration in what is close to him. As do Proust, Huxley (even if his novels are not very satisfactory) and, even though she inserts arbitrary and snobbish elements, Virginia Woolf.

February 12, 1932

It seems almost comical that Paribeni should have taken it upon himself to do the commemoration of Boldini at the Accademia. Boldini did not want to hear even the mention of anything which was Italian; he was like a baptized Jew. And then why annex to Italy a Parisian-Argentine painter, and one who was much more Argentine than Parisian?

Perhaps we three: Nicky,[1] you and I, are the representatives of the end of an epoch; although we differ so greatly
amongst ourselves in age and in education, we are still in a
cycle which one can call either Judaic or Christian or Hellenic, and we partake of it in all of our feelings. Would this
cycle be considered a product of capitalism? It began thou-
sands of years before capitalism was even dreamed of — and
it is the new barbarians, instead, who are excluded from it.
When I see the young Americans who are going into the
studies which are dear to me, I find I shudder; they feel no
human interest in what they are doing — they have the same
distance from it that they would have from chemistry or
osteology.

Lieskov is more Russian and more "historical" than all
the other writers of his country; he makes us participate
more simply in the life of the people, especially their religious life. The Orthodox religion is as much more popular
and domestic than the Catholic as the Catholic is more popular and domestic than the Protestant. To enter into a
Russian Church is a beautiful experience; not here, where
the Russian community is too aristocratic, but, for instance,
in Paris where already there is a Russian "populace." The
sense of brotherhood and intimacy among the faithful, all
conglomerated into the great space where there are not even
any pews, is moving. I ask myself how such a friendly religion can ever decay; despite all those "scientific" efforts
that they are making from the top levels in Russia to extir-

1 Nicky Mariano, Berenson's devoted assistant.

pate it, it must have such very deep and vital roots that it will revive. The fact that the Church is alive in Greece is a good guarantee; the hierarchic order, now destroyed in Russia, will be able to fasten on again to that thread.

February 14, 1932

The Italians have never known how to be historians of Italy, but only good writers of historical monographs or the history of institutions, because they have not been able to discern the kernel of Italian history, which is the Papacy. They have been afraid to confess to themselves the glories and the importance of the Papacy; they have been subdued by the myth of the Risorgimento. A historian like Salvemini would not recognize this defect because Salvemini is not a modern, but an archaic man; which one may deduce from the conditions of his birth, his education, and his life. Besides, Italians have had bad luck as historians in being the only ones among occidentals who have been unable to study the Greeks with relative freedom, because interposed between them and the Greek world is the essentially anti-Hellenic, Jesuit education, and the shadow of the power of Rome.

Two interests are lacking in Croce which prevent him from being the historian that he ought to be; attention to economic conditions and attention to the figurative arts. But is there any historian who satisfies these two conditions (not to speak of all the others)? No, there is not. The modern American historians reduce everything to economic history;

and in any case they would have no artistic material to pay attention to, except literary. Meyer is the best historian of the ancient world, and certainly he keeps his eye on economic reality (he can recount the "diaspora" of the seventh century as vividly as though it were the great navigations and explorations of the Renaissance); he avails himself of the literary texts, but is defective in turning the monuments of the time to account as clear evidence of what Hellenism really is. What is the Greek civilization without its art? Meyer renders the transition to the age of Alexander very well in an intrinsic fashion; he does not attribute the so-called "decadence" to external causes, to the Macedonian and then the Roman invasions, but he sees it as stemming from an internal exhaustion, from exhaustion of the current traditions, from the death of the original impetus; one recalls Croce's references to the "tiredness" of the Baroque age. The impetus ceases when there is no longer any sense of where to apply it—when the occasions are lacking.

Why did the architecture of the seventeenth century flourish throughout all of Italy except for the island of Tuscany? Because it acquired new impetus from the task of "re-clothing" the Counter-Reformation, from marshaling the grand spectacle of the Church's self-rediscovery. It was so much at the forefront that, by contrast, the neighboring arts deteriorated. Painting and sculpture became primarily decorative, subsidiary; they lost their autonomy. It makes me laugh when people nowadays bewail the extraordinary liberties which painting has reacquired, who would like to see the era of "patronage" begin again, of sumptuous commissions delegated to painters. The heaviest rhetoric of Baroque painting stands as evidence of what the result would be.

February 15, 1932

If Fra Angelico had lived in the nineteenth century he would have been another Cézanne. No one comparable to him possesses a "modern" vision of the Florentine landscape; his vision, I say, is modern, though its expression is naturally conditioned by the technique, by the "instrumentation" which was so much less rich and varied at that time. Others can render the Florentine landscape with greater breadth, more panoramically, but his way of feeling the masses and volumes is as contiguous to us as that of Cézanne.

I see in the future a general leveling — a reduction of the tenor of life, an abandonment of luxury; I see the disappearance of fast trains, Palace hotels, ocean liners, all the superfluous things which used to seem necessary signs of well-being; and I see more decency and harmony reigning in everyone. How will this transition occur? Inevitably, almost without anyone's realizing it, by unavoidable necessity, the way it is going on even now, everywhere except in France; but even France will be brought up sharp against necessity and the only possible solution. Administratively we are in a blind alley; our administrative organs were thought out and remodeled at a time when management of affairs amounted to a tenth of what it is today, and the rapidity of communications (which is the multiplying factor) was in much lower proportion; the newest of them date from the French Revolution, and thus are exhausted and by now quite inefficacious. Will an ulterior concentration occur, tending toward a form of state socialism? I don't believe so. I would not like that, but municipal socialism, that is to say socialism which could be easily and rapidly controlled by the community, would seem to me to be opportune. Barriers torn down and relatively small centers enjoying autonomy; this is the future which smiles on me. Do we have to undergo sedition and revolt to arrive at it? Perhaps, but if that is the road, it is well worth it. You and I and a few others would pay with our lives, but this would have no importance for human destiny.

February 16, 1932

People should not be encouraged to take art lightly, but everyone should approach works of art with a sort of timorousness and "holiness." I remember, right from my first encounters with them, how sacred pictures were for me, and how I would set about looking at them in the same spirit that I approached a woman with whom I was in love. Once I was in love, the thing farthest from my mind was to go to bed with the woman; unfortunately she herself or circumstances finally demanded the consummation of that act. Herein lies the superiority of art, which inspires the same sense of love at the beginning but does not lead one on to any act parallel to that of "going to bed." It remains holy forever. When a picture has not given me this sacramental sense I consider it to be not a work of art, but pure diversion — on a par with any music hall spectacle.

How should pictures be hung? With great care as to the placing and spacing, so that as one approaches them one is not chaotic or confused, but disposed toward a sense of reverence; and they should often be rearranged, their positions changed, to avoid their becoming an ordinary and obvious experience for the eye. (You must often change their place, lest they become commonplace.)

March 1, 1932

Eliot is the best of critics when it is a matter of historical or political or economic things, but he becomes deadly when he enters the literary field; then he puts his logic into operation, and his logic operates in such an inexorable manner, with no exit, no salvation, that it reduces everything to an insane asylum. But this is just as it should be: the things of the spirit are not adaptable to formal, mathematical logic; they break such schemes, perforce, and he who does not abandon his schemes is bound to end in the absurd. These are the puritanical limitations which come to the fore in T. S. Eliot.

March 2, 1932

Notwithstanding all the respect and veneration which I have always professed for Morelli, I have to admit that he has remained a dilettante. It is relatively easy and very pleasant to "suck the plums" and then throw away the seeds; I, however, am involved in quite another labor — that of cultivating the entire field which lies before me — of exhausting my argument as much as I can.

When one speaks of artistic individuality one should be reminded that it manifests itself "above and beyond" or really "above and before" style; as a quality of genius, breaking and soaring over rules, or else as pure incompetence, unable to master them. Along the embankments of "style" remain people who have no individuality, who are purely academic. By the word "style" I mean here the mere form or formula which is dominant; one can also mean, by style, the personal quality of the artist, but then for the sake of clarity it is better to say personal style. Individuality, even the individuality of deficiency, does count; it is something more than pure stylistic bravura; it has a vaster and more distant horizon, albeit perhaps confused and as yet unattained.

What matters in Poliziano is the fusion which he achieves between the naturalness of popular poetry and his own humanistic erudition: perfect. To a foreigner like myself the result seems marvelous; he alone of the Italian poets manages to preserve the grace and beauty of the "rispetti" and "stornelli" which leave us with our mouths agape, though the Italians don't seem to be aware of it. Italians seem suffocated by what always becomes rhetoric in the great qualities of their past masters of poetry; from Petrarch, one can say, all the way to D'Annunzio. Poliziano is an isolated case who comes closer to certain foreigners: to the poets of the Pléiade, or to Ronsard before he became too elaborate and cultivated; with overtones of English poets (Burns, Keats) and above all with a kinship to Heine. In Du Bellay there are domestic, affectionate overtones which are totally lacking in Petrarch.

Totally? I would say yes; for even in the sonnets, which derive their inspiration from an immediate scene and which are more separate from the "corpus" of Laura, there is something more rounded, something broader and emptier — there is not that direct simplicity in which nothing reverberates after the initial sound, and which nevertheless, as one listens to it at length, creates song. Poliziano belongs to the fifteenth century Renaissance: the paintings of Fra Angelico, of Filippo Lippi, Botticelli's "Primavera." I mean the "quality" of those paintings, and not so much that his descriptions are figurative. This is true of other poets; and of who more than Dante? With Dante, of course, the incision is deep. But in Poliziano we have the scene by itself, and in Dante and in others so many other things enter beyond the simple description of the scene. But what greatness there is in Dante's scenes! The "sounds" that are sung in Paradise! If only there were not all that theology and all that trite Florentine chronicle surrounding it!

There is no history without polemic, without an axe to grind, without originating in antagonism to something which exists and which it wants to combat and substitute. So much of my work is polemic, and so much of that has now lost its meaning and importance because it was directed against attitudes and against fashions which by now are defunct (and in great part defunct thanks to my work itself), and now so many people have exaggerated my polemical role that I really should repolemicize against them to set them right again.

Cubism's effort to reveal massive, square, heavy forms and internal bone and nerve structures is an effort to abstract a quality which is present in all works of art, but is usually "incorporated" in them, and conditioned by many other values. Similarly the "descriptive" or "sculptural" quality in Poliziano's work is less powerful but more imposing than, let's say, in Dante, because in Dante it does not stand alone, but is accompanied and enriched by so many other qualities.

March 3, 1932

An explanation of why, in the past, I have thought of attributing "La Bella Simonetta"[1] to Ghirlandaio would require a whole volume. Little by little I am more and more convinced by the "Botticellism" of Ghirlandaio, and to whom should that painting be attributed if not to an eminent Botticellian? It is not a first-rate picture, but neither should it be assigned to a painter who lacks personality. And it is not Botticelli. The "line" is not Botticellian: it is too sharp, and it is flat — it does not model anything. In Botticelli the line, though very nervous, suggests the volume and really shapes it all by itself.

March 5, 1932

I know what the great defect of my writing is: rhythm. My phrases follow one another in quick succession too pressingly, almost "saccadées" because I get transported by my

---

[1] In the Condé Museum at Chantilly. In the 1932 catalogues it is marked as a work by Piero di Cosimo.

haste and anxiety to say the things that I feel so urgently; I have never known how to give my rhythm time to expand. Thus no matter how much it may correspond to certain of my intentions, it lacks suaveness. But the "corrections" which Mary, as much as Logan and Trevy[2] continually make in my prose have not taught me anything; they have only threatened to sterilize me completely, and if I have reacted, and have gone on writing, it simply means that the things within me were pressing me and I had to express them.

March 6, 1932

Doesn't an orchestra conductor get tired of repeating the performance of the same masterpieces millions of times throughout his whole life? No, certainly not; every performance is a novelty and an adventure; furthermore nobody with any imagination gets tired of reading and rereading "their" classics, just as I do not get tired of seeing the same painting, in the original or in photographs. Impressions are never "exhausted"; they are reborn freshly every time. At the utmost I have experienced a momentary "saturation" for certain paintings, for certain painters, or, for that matter, for certain forms of art; but this comes almost as a nervous state — almost in order to make room for other more urgent interests. And very shortly thereafter I recover the interest I had lost. As for a historical interest in a work of art, I deny that it can be disassociated from the aesthetic one; paintings carry with them so much of the environment

[2] The writer, Logan Pearsall Smith, B.B.'s brother-in-law, and his friend, the poet R. C. Trevelyan.

from which they were produced. But by expanding its particular historical interest one arrives at a better understanding of the beauty of a work of art, and thus from contact with new forms of beauty one's taste is expanded. Many works which first perhaps offended me now interest me because they contribute to "filling the void," to furnishing me with the documentation which serves to complete my historical sense of art, but then later I discover in these very works the beauty, the particularity, which makes them excel among others similar to them, whereas I would never have supposed it had I not bothered to look at them. Thus one becomes more eclectic, or better to say more universal.

It is historically ascertained that the derivation of all ornamental motifs come from the lotus: from the flower, from the bud, from the stalk, and from the plant sections. One could propose many other natural origins for various ornamental forms and figures, but they do not link up with historical data. The evolution of forms of the lotus can be followed step by step from Egypt to the present, and even forms which seem to be derived from elsewhere can be quickly traced to it. The acanthus, for example, which is not properly a copy of the acanthus leaf but is a half palm which came to be the same thing. Everything begins in Egypt, except a few sporadic manifestations which are not worth bringing up. Men are lacking in the spirit of observation, and the imitation of natural things — that is, the selection of them by imitation of them — is always an extraordinary flash of genius. The

Egyptians experimented, and chose the lotus; afterwards ornamental forms became complex, deriving one from the other, sometimes varying through mere incompetence in the reproduction. The Minoan age had another form: the vine shoot — "dog's flight" as the Germans call it. When it became geometric it gave rise to the "Greek" form, and as it went on to be repeated in profusion — not freely any longer but within a closed space — it gave rise, in successive imprints, to Moslem ornamentation and to all filigree work.

Architecture tends toward a compromise between invention's free play of movement, and geometricization, which constrains it in balance and rhythm. Tired and decadent epochs lose the inventive sense and tend to isolate the geometric and rhythmic element, as one sees in Cubism.

March 8, 1932

Boast is always a cry of despair, except when in the young it is a cry of hope.

Gangsters are a body without tradition, which means they are always ready to break their internal ties and wreak slaughter among themselves; in this they differ very much from the Mafia and from the Camorra which have lasted for centuries, comporting themselves before the outside world with perfect correctness, and keeping internal discord quiet through a policy of silence, like the Jesuits. Besides, gangsters are part and parcel of the provisionality of American life; they are the legitimate descendants of the pioneer spirit. "Pioneering" in America gives no support to administrative procedure, and looks in every case for the more expedient way. A sense of justice can be left to countries which have time to waste, it is an obstacle in dynamic, "Fordian" nations.

The sovereign sin of woman is to be too logical, while a man's greatest quality is being able to leave off the armament of logic when it is a matter of making contact with reality. Thus women, in men's professions, would spoil everything by following questions to their extreme consequences. It is not true that woman is fickle; women turn in a circle, always around one center, whereas a man can truly displace himself — can live in space.

March 10, 1932
There are no intellectually sincere conversions to Catholicism, or any other revealed religion. Whoever has once abandoned the world of magic (and I do not say it is a world to depreciate; I recognize its fascination, its merits, and its power) cannot go back to it, unless in a case of mental deficiency or disease. People of today can be born into it and stay there all their lives; that is quite another condition. Scientists, mathematicians, can accept it because they do not try to control its principles; but he who is acquainted with a life of thought, no. Literary converts are among the insincere ones; sometimes they are seeking new notoriety, sometimes seeking emotions or arguments to pull themselves along; the need to write, to express oneself, is such (it is a

"kakosethos" [1]) that when they have exhausted their own possibilities they would be willing to attach themselves to sky hooks. If anyone really wanted to join the Catholic religion he should approach it through Saint Thomas. Saint Thomas is a man of sincere thinking and is sincerely Catholic, because he lived in a time when it was impossible to leave the world of magic — magic of the Church, Moslem magic, or the magic of Julian the Apostate, and Porphyrius. The Greek world had worn itself out in these patterns which were different but all equally magical. The absolute necessity of religious imagination was such that the atheists of the Middle Ages, who did exist, are not interesting because they are too much outside and against the current. Only in the young do I see any possibility for "return" today: in those young people who are under the illusion, as they talk, of having left the Church, because they have been enjoined to do so by others, and who, when they turn to her, find their true being. It is characteristic of young people, in fact, to take on their convictions by ear, and to proclaim thoughts and faiths of which they are not really persuaded; so the act of sincerity is the one which takes them to the opposite pole. There is no need to place any trust in a man's opinions before he is forty, not because he is insincere, but because he is too rich in possible ideas, too much at the mercy of chaos and confusion.

March 15, 1932

All the superstitions inherited from the Hellenic world were concentrated in Byzantium; its artists continually tried

[1] A cursed custom, a cursed condemnation.

to return to the Greek ideal of beauty, and the development of Byzantine art lies in this series of "attempts." In reality one can say that all art after the "death" of the Greek world consists in successive rebirths, achieved with more or less success, up to the full vitality of the Italian Renaissance.

Neo-Catholics carry around their thought as though it were a squirrel in a cage — the medieval world was a cage, but ours is one no longer and no one can continue in this fashion. The "sense of sin" is also a matter peculiar to converts, beginning with Barbey and passing from Bourget to Mauriac. The ancient Catholics were immune to it.

March 17, 1932

To develop a taste for painting, only one form of teaching is possible: looking at them until the painting has penetrated into you and constitutes part of your soul. It is the "form of teaching," if one can call it thus, which I have used with Mary, only indicating to her at the very most which pictures to look at and which she could leave alone — the only legitimate teaching. And I too learned in this way. I was taught nothing except the following: old paintings are dreadful and should be scorned. This is what my painter friends said, being even more disdainful then than they are today of all past art, and I myself was not even prepared or predisposed in any particular way toward painting; if anything it was toward Greek sculpture. But once I reached Paris I passed entire days at the Louvre, stopped dead in front of the paintings, until I had to lean on the railings which protected them in order to keep from falling. I learned to know them one by one and to recall them in my memory in the order they were hung in the galleries, and thus they began to work within me. And Greek sculpture as well, for one field of acquaintance cannot mature without the other. I began to write only when I believed I knew more about the subject than anyone else who had ever existed — a gross illusion on my part, no doubt.

April 30, 1932

Barocci paints like Marie Laurencin; it is interesting to find Marie Laurencin in the sixteenth century. All the painters of the late Renaissance, the "mannerists," excel in portraits; they fall down, however, when they attempt composition, because of a sort of mania for anything new. They tried so hard to vary the traditional poses in pictures with religious subjects — depicted so many times by the great masters — that they finally exhausted, so to speak, all possible variation. From this is derived their "genre" — forced and rhetorical.

Landscape comes to us from the north — from the Flemish and their French contemporaries. In Italy on the other hand the emphasis was on the "view" — the background and the air behind the painting. But in earlier times — in the fifteenth century — there were masters of the attenuated landscape in Italy also, who rendered the naked forms of the hills and their sterile line. We have seen, in fact, that Cézanne had a colleague in Piero della Francesca, and it is since

Cézanne that Piero has been considered great. For it has always taken contemporary interest to shed light on forgotten art.

May 4, 1932

Tolstoy is gigantic, but he is not titanic. He is not in rebellion, or if he is, he is only in rebellion against his own sex, not against life in general. He loves life right to the end. His rebellion, and his religious impetus, is that of a boy at dawn after a night of carousing — the morning after. He remained a boy until the age of eighty, which is a great sign of force. It means that he would have needed eight hundred years to live — or at least that he would have had the wherewithal to fill them.

The music of Richard Strauss is like ventilated Wagner.

May 5, 1932

Were the great Italian painters also "great souls"? They were perfect artisans, but there are no signs of the power of their intellects and their internal lives outside of their paintings. Michelangelo's is a terrible soul. Botticelli is a very sensitive soul who "feels" the beauty of the human figure in all his most minute touches. To see all his drawings again, as I am doing at this moment, makes me realize the unfailing perfection of his contours, even in drawings which do fail when taken as a whole. Abstracting the single figure from the composition, they possess an exquisite decorative quality, the like of which has never been seen. It is wrong to compare them to Japanese figures, because they are too superior. The Greeks possessed love for the proportions of the human body, but it was already an abstract and intellectualistic love; with him, on the other hand, it is the sign, the movement, the vibration of the line which counts, which lives on its own without any need of transposition and measure.

May 6, 1932

The finale of *War and Peace* is absolutely necessary to the book. It is like the Aristotelian "hule"; it is the reprise of peaceful life after the heroic years. In the same way the best Renaissance buildings go with the most hard and severe forms: basilican forms, for example, with short volutes which unite and soften them. "Fatality" is present in the whole book: in the culminating moments as well as in the most tranquil moments. Man confronted by Fate: this is the essence of tragedy. In *Anna Karenina* the Fate is disproportionate; one senses right from the beginning what Anna's end must be. That ending is not necessary — it is like taking advantage of one's nerves. And if we find ourselves taking into consideration that in Anna's society it is necessary, it means that that society is dead for us and that the novel reflects it in too temporary an aspect.

Rome: June 4, 1932

These bas-reliefs — "The Birth of Venus[1]" — are both archaic and elegant. They are like the Parmigianino of archaism. They seem like contemporary copies rather than

[1] In the Terme Museum.

originals — the weakness of their execution in certain points betrays the copyist. As though the forms were not "felt" in their full relief, but were, in fact, copied from a model in which they had been felt, and so had degenerated, in certain passages, to something trite and linear. Copies are always like this. The authenticity is countersigned more than anything else by the equality of value which permeates all the work, not by the perfection of the details; by the fact that the copyist no longer recognized the work's formal identity, and so could not recreate it.

The arms of the *Moses*[1] are muscular but graceful; the rest — torso, head, beard and feet, are those of a gigantic river god: no mystery in the conception but a great marine form clothed in a profluvium of algae. The tablets of the Law dwindle. But the gracefulness of the arms, attached to those great shoulders and to those great hands, is already so much a sign of the Baroque! It is a contrast which the classical age would not have borne. The representation becomes more powerful and persistent, but the secret of the proportion is lost, and Michelangelo found he had become separated irremediably from this. He was unable to finish the monument. Once Moses was done it lost all interest for him. He followed that inspiration decades later in the *Last Judgment*.

June 5, 1932

We — people of my age — grew up with a feudal idea of liberty as the power of the individual, which had been

[1] In San Pietro in Vincoli.

subjugated under Louis XIV but had remained alive in men's spirits. It is certain that economic conditions and, one might almost say, topographical conditions, limited that type of liberty. Only a few millionaires are allowed it today, and for how long? What subsists instead, and is an irrepressible requisite, is freedom of speech — the word and the press. It is almost a physiological need; wherever it is suppressed one finds tyranny. Tyranny which cannot last: that repressed need ferments and in some almost pathological way it is bound to manifest itself.

June 7, 1932

Egyptian columns of the Imperial Age, with a frieze of figures at the base. The shape of the relief, in the very hard material, is very gentle. It makes me think of Latin poetry. Perhaps an Italian could not feel the contrast which I feel between the language, which I find very hard and very rough as compared with Greek, and the unusually light vibration in certain words.

June 9, 1932

Bernini is classical. He does not belong to the Renaissance, he belongs to Classicism, because he accomplishes and realizes that toward which the classical masters tended. With Bernini the sculpture and architecture of Pergamo find expression, after a long interval. The "formula" of classical art is taken up again in the Renaissance and finds its logical outlet in Bernini. In the same way the Turkish mosques are the development and the fulfillment of Santa Sofia; Santa Sofia

broke the Byzantine architectonic current, and it is taking
the energy of a new people and conditions of different times
for it to begin again, in the same place, at the point where it
stopped. Popular energy helps the development of forms
of art, but it does not determine them: it lies dormant for
centuries in the same place, like a vein of gold, until new miners come to disinter it.

The real interest of my life, or at least of my youth, has
been poetry; until my thirties I did not read prose except for
study or for information, and read even this type of prose
fairly seldom. Poems, on the other hand, I read exten-
sively, and the problem which was with me every day was of
severing off what counted in poetry and distinguished it
from mere versification. Then, all of a sudden, it seemed to
me that this problem was resolved by the figurative arts,
and, more particularly, by painting, because with painting
I would have my "object" firmly before my eyes, not fluid and
mobile and in a certain sense delusive, as it was in verses. So
I started to study painting intensively, with the secret
hope of turning to poetry some day, and the skeleton of my
thinking on the subject of poetry may be found set down in
certain notes which I wrote about twenty or twenty-five
years ago — saved for whomever will want to write my
"paralipomeni." [1] — Is poetry an art superior to others, or is
music or painting superior? — I don't understand the meaning of the question. So long as they are adopted with the same
intensity of conviction, the arts are of equal worth, and a
"scale" of arts can only be of interest as autobiographical

1 These notes have not been found among Berenson's papers.

data. If anyone — and many people do, in fact — happens to place music at the top it is because the artistic element in music is more easily distinguishable; music actually does not "represent" and it does not "narrate." The narrative unity of a poem does not at all go hand in hand with its artistic unity: Poe is right to a great extent when he says that every epic is too long to be poetry. The "minor arts" are justly called minor because their brevity and their minuteness do not permit that they be fully expressive; there is something artificial about them, a reduced proportion which is not naturally suited to the state of mind, the intention, which motivates expression. Cerebral or abstract forms are just as artificial, such as those many attempts at art seen in recent times, which answer a need for novelty at all costs. Art requires a human language, and should follow not a convention, but the given factors of the strict relationship between our psychology and physiology and the external world; so long as this relationship does not change we can rest assured that, in essence, art will not change. Architecture, for example, although not wholly representative of what I have in mind, corresponds to a certain sense of symmetry and proportion which is born in our bodies, and to a psychological need to "de-chaotize" space. An immense space can become harmonious through a work of architecture. And there is a strong tie with music. We derive pleasure and satisfaction from so many other objects and factors: from well-polished surfaces, from color tones, from the unravelling of lines, but this is not the same as that sense of the fullness of art which comes only from meaningful, impregnated form, and which requires the conviction of the artist.

June 16, 1932

Painting in seventeenth century Italy was nothing more than decoration; then in the eighteenth century there was real painting again — whenever the subject was not religious. But in the seventeenth century there was nothing but the astounding and the rhetorical. This is not true of the other countries: France, with Poussin and Claude Lorrain, and Spain. Velásquez is the only great Spanish artist (as Cervantes is their only great poet) but he is greater than the best of his contemporaries and masters. The other Spaniards are occasionally forceful, but so much inferior to even the mediocre Italians! El Greco was taken up by Spain; he was not Spanish — his origin is Cretan, which is to say Byzantine. His formation was entirely Italian, but in Spain he found the air which suited him, and met with no brake on his inclinations. He would never have painted as he did had he remained in Venice. Philip II, however, did not appreciate him. When he saw the sample sketches he would not approve of El Greco decorating the cloister of the Escorial; the examples of Titian were too close. But in Toledo he developed fully, and by now he has become identified with that city which was not his own. The Spaniards sin against taste. This is not true of Velásquez or of a sculptor like Montañés, who stretch to the limits of taste but do not breach it.

June 17, 1932

The modern examples of architecture seem to me to be amusing more than anything else — born of mental ingenuity, that is, rather than the aesthetic sense: objects created by one mentality to provide amusement for another. I see no beauty in it, and I do not see that there can be any beauty in the future. We lack today, with our use of cement, any sense of resistance of material; and in general, where the material does not resist there is no longer any art. Cement is like cardboard, giving way in any direction, and adaptable to every use. It is outstandingly serviceable and so will continue to be adopted in construction, and this does mean that things will be well-constructed even if they are simple. But these will be buildings, not architecture and not art. Geometrical proportion will be easily reached, and so, if you like, will harmony, but it will be simply the harmony which exists in any problem whatever which has been resolved. Art should break the bonds of material. Already the examples we are familiar with have arrived at precisely this simplicity; they serve their purpose. Or when they are of inferior quality (like the American skyscrapers) they manage, just barely, to create a festive, scenic effect.

Emilio Cecchi is the Italian version of Arthur Symons; he is the heir to the English "fin de siècle" spirit, to the literary descendants of Wilde and of Pater. As was true of them, it is the negative aspect which counts in his taste, over and above his exclusive and recondite admiration for some things — a spirit of destructive and reactionary criticism. He always finds excellent reasons for not appreciating certain masterpieces. He is a man of imagination and whims, and so am I, but I do try to reason and test my whims rather than abandon myself to them. I try to see if they measure up to the comparison of other impressions which I know to be well founded, or, even more, of my own critical ideas. I continually make appeal from Philip the Drunk to Philip the Sober.

August 16, 1932

D. H. Lawrence bores me very quickly. His contrary attitude — aggressive toward anything which is not pure instinctive force and warmth — to me seems uninteresting and barbaric. Huxley admires him, but I think it is a passing infatuation, caused by his attraction to a force and warmth which he himself lacks; and he does not understand (for the time being) that an intelligence like his own must be able to do without them, or at best that he must preserve his mastery of them in order to guide them.

The English, who have an excellent palate for poetry, are quite deprived of one as far as food is concerned.

August 17, 1932

From the moment that a person leaves me, even the dearest and most intimate, like Nicky and Mary, I forget their particular characteristics and they become for me like historical characters whom I know thoroughly but not through any direct knowledge — not by way of the particular and minute and irrelevant mannerisms of everyday life. I believe in the historicity of people more than in their momentary and fleeting expressions, more than in their extreme and flimsy individualism. So it is not important to me to know writers, thinkers, living artists; I know them better in their work, and reaching some ulterior "knowledge" of them would require that I spend too long a time in their company. I do not believe in interviews for this same reason. And superficial acquaintance is excessively delusive, particularly with the great writers and poets. Matthew Arnold, who used to dine with Logan, could do nothing but ask him information about his worldly acquaintances, and insulted him by saying: "Don't you know Lord X? Oh, you will soon meet him, certainly." You could not discuss anything with George Moore. Artists preserve their capacity for creation and are tone deaf in mutual encounters.

The communism in the Bible — the repartition of land and the remission of debts every few years — is a false communism, that is to say it is a sincere aspiration without any basis in law and in custom, and it is the beginning of utopia. Communism truly is the primitive form of society, but at that time it is unconscious. In the Jews the vein of indignation was and always is very alive: the prophet Amos, who was a contemporary of Hesiod, hurls invective and rends his garments over conditions of the poor which the Greek poet describes and laments quietly, as an inevitable grief. One finds the same cry in Karl Marx, at least in the Communist Manifesto.

What is English cant? It is the firm and obstinate belief in certain principles, and the inability to imagine a practice of life which contradicts them. So the English "cantists," no matter what their actions and their conduct may be, do not perceive any dissent between their conduct and the principle in which they believe, even when it is as plain as day. The hypocrite is conscious of what he is concealing, but that type of Englishman is ignorant of it; therefore he possesses an aggressive, tremendous, good faith, which produces disastrous results and makes any accommodation impossible.

Excessive sincerity produces "mannerisms" when it involves a concentration of thought and detachment from others; and it is all too easy for excessive sincerity to involve this, precisely because it is worthy and exclusive. The sincere man does not pay any attention to any other mode of being, and thus keeps on blindly accentuating "his" way, until others begin to recognize it as an unpleasant peculiarity and accuse him of being "affected." But affectation is another thing. There are extremely sincere — even excessively sincere — artists like Botticelli and Crivelli who are clearly mannered, or mannerist, but nobody would say that their painting is an affectation.

August 18, 1932

What has happened in Russia? A "geometricization" of individuals, a greater coarsening than that which is noticeable in other countries; the death of a ruling class and the blossoming of the masses, to whom images, myths and projects which make sense to them are directly addressed. The Five-Year Plan works this way. The geometricization first revealed itself in art with Cubism, then in life, then in politics; it is a descent into barbarism. It will be barbarism without any profound wreckage or subversion, without any emigration of people, because there is no longer any place to migrate; and it will not even endure, furthermore, because there remain abundant monuments and documents from the past and present, and besides (the only thing which counts), the technical capacity to decipher them also remains. In the Dark Ages there were monuments, but people no longer knew how to look at them, no longer knew how to read the documents, so they disappeared completely from the general consciousness and a rebirth was necessary. Today the diffusion of knowledge acts in some way as a guarantee: the revival will occur more quickly, let us say in one or two centuries. And in Russia it has to occur — fomented by the very texts on which Bolshevism is founded — by the reading matter of the proletariat who will rediscover bygone times and their civil tradition in these writings.

August 19, 1932

Men are unable to resist the attraction of machines. If an automobile could have been presented to Plato, Plato would have become Ford.

August 21, 1932

One cannot say that an abundance of questions is an indication of great culture; it is a sign of great adolescence in the most serious and seasoned people, and occurs often among the Americans, who remain unadult for their whole lives. Boys know how to ask the most embarrassing questions, with a great deal of naïve malice, but this does not mean that they are cultivated or wise. One should be able to resist both the desire to ask and the impatience to respond.

A terrible crisis occurred in the fourth century — a real suspension of the civilized world which became unable to pay attention to anything except the resolution of one problem: that of the Trinity. Nobody knew what to tell themselves, but they all felt that until this was resolved life could not regain its regular rhythm. Today we are in a time of crisis once again; that is to say there is at least a Trinity of economic problems which have not been resolved and which occupy and blur our horizon. We see how money behaves, but we know nothing of its nature, and we worry about its future. And what can be expected from governments, with regard to economy? Only in exceptional times — very fluid, plastic times — can the government give a push, make the economy move in a given direction; usually it has no control. Coming out of a crisis means having resolved a vital problem, which then will seem very simple and perhaps even nonexistent.

1919 was a "plastic" year in which it was possible to remodel history; unfortunately bad influences had the upper hand. And one cannot even lay serious blame on the European statesmen, who were really prisoners of the phantoms which they themselves had evoked, and of the Frankenstein monster — propaganda — constructed for practical reasons during the war, but by then insatiable and imperious. Lloyd George was the servant of his electors, whom he had unleashed; Clemenceau of a chauvinist patriotism which the war had exacerbated; Sonnino of a pigheaded territorial hunger. But the really guilty, diabolical one was Henry Cabot Lodge. It was he who undermined the ground behind Wilson and by superseding his authority in America made it impossible for him to take any action whatever in Paris. Probably he only ruined the situation through hatred of Wilson, through a desire for personal affirmation which bore no relation to any political aims.

The Medici were Maecenases? The Medici, rather, were the dominators and in some way strangulators of Florence. Florence had experienced the accumulation of energies which overflowed into many branches and fertilized various territories all through the thirteenth and fourteenth centuries; and if this particular family of merchants had not become preponderant, probably the progress of Florence, under the concerted direction of numerous families, would have been freer and more enduring. I do know that instead of encouraging Leonardo's art they encouraged his flight, and that he then found other Maecenases in Milan — the Sforzas, who hired him as a hydraulic engineer. Those few paintings which he did go on to paint were the start of a scourge: the "Leonardesque school," which emphasized solely his grace of execution; sweetening it to the point of unverisimilitude. Maecenases do not play any part in the development of civilization. They too, at the very most, are a sign of the energy accumulated in those happy moments which constitute the apex of a civilization; they represent a phenomenon parallel to this — one might almost say an effect of it, and certainly not its cause at all. Civilization is actually the accumulation of energy occurring in a lean period; one sees this definition very clearly in Egyptian history. One of the great "lean periods" is the so-called "Middle Ages," from the fourth to the tenth centuries. At that point everything was extinguished; life retreated from the cities, commerce was reduced to a heavy form of exchange in natural produce, and the few movements which caught fire did not find any kindling, like the brief Carolingian civilization. Even the Arab phenomenon is proof of a thin civilization. In order for the movement of Mohammed to succeed, the ecumenical world had to be reduced to a desert. Other Mohammeds had proved themselves many times before him, but they had met with too much resistance on all sides.

One myth expels another, and the myth of the present is no less "mythical" than yesterday's; this is true, but there is a way out, and it lies in the creation of personal conviction, detached from the myths which are public and common convictions. Personal conviction may be superstitious but it is not mythical unless a community — one might say a psychological rather than territorial community — participates in it. The myth is born as the creation of a few, and becomes integrated very slowly. If we consider Christianity as a myth, we see that it went on being integrated until the sixteenth century, since the Reformation did not dissolve it but really revived its vigor by injecting Nordic roughness into it, as an antidote to the Roman refinement which tried to constrain it in theology — constrain it, that is, in a rationalization which tended to extinguish it altogether. Whoever attaches himself strongly to "new concepts" of the world, and expects revelations and new forms of life from them, is ready for a new myth and desirous of it. Like everyone in Rome before the advent of Christianity, who already knew that the Homeric myth was dead and were running after any occult novelty which came from Asia.

I reproach Freud for being an uncultured man, with no philosophic training, with no historical and universal cognizance of things. A Jew from the ghetto.

August 22, 1932
The effect which a performance (or the reading of a novel) has on me is overpowering. I remember one time when I was taken to see (without realizing it) not a noble tragedy but one of those dramas which excoriate the social structure in front of the audience; I think it was *La Robe Rouge*, wherein the inadaptability of the law to individual cases is rendered, complete with evidence. Well, for a month I used to wake up in the night with nightmares about the violence of those scenes.

Friendship leads to familiarity, which is something quite different from intimacy. It is a familiarity which rises above intimate things precisely because it is the handiwork of life led almost in common; of common interests, of common assumptions about our motives and sentiments. Married life leads to this familiarity also; but intimacy, it seems to me, is born between the man and woman who are very much attracted to one another but who must live at a distance, so those momentary encounters occur in which every mystery is dissipated and every secret confided — that lifting of every veil, which will last only a second, but which gives you a sense of the deepest possible understanding. Between men, something hinders it; intimacy is a wound. With a woman you know that the weapon or the act which wounds also heals, but not between men; they inflict useless wounds on each other and then are mortified by the offense they have inflicted and the offense they have received.

I very quickly get tired of women who enter into a man's life and take on everything from him; who allow twenty-four hours of acquaintance to change their judgment, their scope, their aspirations, and their values. I want women to live in my universe, but to have independence, to have personal reactions. Furthermore they disgust me when I discover that there have been great blots left by men who have preceded me. I say blots because they are not ideas or sentiments consonant with their own souls, diffused in them so as to have become personal; and it is still worse when, as often occurs, they have been produced by men whom I scorn.

The amnesia of women astounds me, and puts me off from them. It is a physiological phenomenon which is not lack of memory but real innocence: complete ignorance with respect to antecedent facts, and almost always with respect to an entire relationship with a man. It is this phenomenon which enables them to lead so many separate lives — each one new, without any passage from one to the next.

It seems a sin to me that two such uncultivated writers as Shaw and Wells should have the greatest influence in England. Shaw is more intelligent, but both are so lacking in humanity, lacking in "pietas," taking no pains over history, from whence, after all, their reforming genius, their Utopian mania, come. Having no knowledge of the past, they have no knowledge of the future. They conceive of a static, fixed, future — a beautiful blue sky over men's heads which goes hand in hand with beautiful days and ought never again to be shaken by bad weather. They are full of fury and have no sense of being patient with the future of humanity, because they have not learned any lessons about it from the past.

August 23, 1932
The nineteenth century was a century of controversies which were conducted, however, with a sort of periodic ferocity, as though it were all a question of a game; innovators and traditionalists faced each other like two teams, with a strict dialectic of precise formulas which were conventions and nothing else; it was one great golf match. History begins beyond philology, as it does beyond apologetics. History could begin now.

The essence of the beautiful. In my opinion, if you begin investigating you find the good at the root of the beautiful, just as you find the beautiful at the root of the good. It is a fusion which shapes the meaning of human destiny — the beautiful (and good) being that which does not contradict but which aids and abets human destiny; a "quid" then, which encompasses within itself the heroic and the tragic. Even the common people feel this desire, and it follows that the beautiful is a thing eminently to be desired. But people are likewise quick to make mistakes and to run after false harbingers of beauty: falsely mythical works which seem to be pervaded by a great heroic impulse and to be full of destiny. These are the most easily translatable. I think of Ibsen, who has something false about him, and of that completely false Galsworthy.

Beyond, and for me much higher, there is the beauty of "type" which is like the manifestation and the fixation of a myth. Vermeer is the consummate example as a painter, and Jane Austen as a writer, of this form of art. Rite, in the sense of ecstasy in action. It is like an energy spent with no set purpose, trying neither to teach nor to reform. It occurs at the culmination of culture. The whole eighteenth century experienced this spontaneous beauty; people setting out naturally, almost unconsciously, to "recite." The pomp of Louis XIV, like Arcadia and like the Rousseauism of the court ladies. They were ritual acts, like the Mass, which is Divine Comedy — representing the Passion of Christ in daily repetition. And perhaps ritual elements can be found today in sports, although here for the most part the energy is pure exuberance, without any wider significance.

When a literary work is like a compact sphere then, it seems to me, one is not aware of its "realism" — at least not as a defect. I think of realism as those points which break the surface of the sphere: dates and persons which are not encompassed, but remain extraneous, in too strong relief, so that they wound and offend the reader.

August 24, 1932

Chekhov delineates his world in relief above a universal landscape; he separates his world, but does not close it off; and the shadow which weighs down over him is circumscribed with light. So his air is not oppressive. Alvaro and Moravia, or other Italian writers of today, create a sense of oppressiveness precisely because they do not enter into that universal current which is the true artistic current. Katherine Mansfield takes everything from Chekhov; not just, though it is most evident, the best of her stories, but also the best of her letters, which are pale in comparison with Chekhov's correspondence.

August 25, 1932

The unity of the thirteenth century was nothing at all compared with what exists today. Today social and economic pressures oblige everyone to comport themselves according to precise and restricted norms, in a sort of vice which is much more powerful than that of religion. Though the virginity of the Madonna may not be of any importance to anyone, everyone's hackles are quick to rise over the dogmas of economics; everyone hastens to smell out and stone the "bolshevik" under no matter what form of aberrant thought;

they are all ready to immolate themselves in defense of the state, in spite of the fact that the modern state is the first institution to become bolshevik: it is chief among those who, with taxes, with inflation, with conversions into stock, make attempts on the life of the economy and subsequently on private liberty.

August 26, 1932

Boredom is the cement of nice people's houses. Nice people have to go to the theater in order to entertain themselves.

August 27, 1932

The Irish are animals who cannot put up with a single "archy" and who cannot be governed in any way, except by superstitious poets, as the ancient Celts were by the Druids. They flee from any "centrality" whatsoever, even if it be that of pure intellect — that cultural "center" which classicism denotes. Anyone who is impassioned by them is a rebel against civilization.

August 29, 1932

Tiepolo: a great decorator. He is not a great painter. He is like the Metastasio of painting. If someone sees him as being greater it means that he does not know what real painting is.

August 30, 1932

As time goes along India repulses me more and more, as being a mastodon of chaos. It is Ireland multiplied by one hundred. It is a country which understands none of our values, and is even further from us than Japan or China.

Why are people not content to know that things "are," but have to ask where they come from and where they are going? Nobody's thinking stops at the presence of things, at their itness. Christianity revolts entirely against this "it" toward a future hope, and furthermore whatever there is of the earthly in Christianity — moral stoicism, Aristotelianism — was all already present in Hellenism. Human stomachs went on to digest primitive Christianity because men will digest anything and pursue their lives without any extraordinary changes.

December 13, 1932

Mathematics is pure mental creation, founded, however, on premises which are not repugnant to intellect. The premises of theology, on the other hand, are not reasonable. But even in mathematics what offended me most, from the time I was very young, were the axioms. If I had not had to do my sums with axioms I would have become a proven mathematician.

Culture consists above all in that which is forgotten.

December 14, 1932

Inside Baudelaire there rumbles, or grumbles, all of medieval Latin poetry. This echo of poetry which he remakes into poetry, attracts me more than anything else about him. Many, however, who are bewildered by certain "novelties" in Baudelaire, would have to shift the object of their amazement if they knew his sources. What is more beautiful, from a certain point of view, than the Dies Irae, or the Stabat Mater?

Where does that special tenderness come from in Latin poetry? A caress, a liquefaction — think of the *Pervirgilium Veneris* — which runs between the structure of the hexameters the more correct, armed, and precise that they are. How can one ever say what it comes from? From Greek poetry? But Latin poetry is Greek poetry — the same thing exactly, with the instrument changed, that being the language. One would do better to say that Greek poetry changes, is renovated, experiences another youth, when at a certain point it comes to be written in Latin; that it needs this new opportunity in order to return to life.

In the fifteenth century the Church humanized itself: those mystical, popular movements which in the fourteenth century had seemed to be at its center, to constitute its essence, had been expelled from its bosom to the fringes and on outside; it knew the splendor of the Papacies of Julius II and of Leo X. But the popular movement, too strong to be denied and repressed, was scattered abroad among the most uncultivated people, who were horrified by the "paganization" and demanded a reason for it. The Reformation is a survival of medieval instincts. So is the Counter-Reformation, inasmuch as it looks to the Reformation. But then the Reformation had to suppress the haughty attacks of the petty, intemperate populace; it had its own dissidents, iconoclasts and reformers. It became humanized and organized at its center, only to be constantly more attacked and eaten away by the implacable elements on the periphery: the Puritans, the commoners, the medievalists of Protestantism. So that today the extreme limits of Protestantism, the most recent and momentary sects — the Salvation Army, for example — border much more closely on the heroic era of the religious middle ages than the Papacy does.

December 15, 1932

The Communists of twenty years ago are moderate socialists today; the socialists of twenty years ago are bourgeois today; this proves that the bourgeoisie is very much of an anthropological institution which is the common and almost indispensable destiny of the mature man.

When Eleanora Duse came to unburden her confidences after being abandoned by D'Annunzio, she was a touching and repellent spectacle. Never would I have imagined such utter animality in her. This utter animality was precious, for any fire, any élan, in a person partakes of animality; but that there should be so much astounded me. I had seen her play all parts, even the part of absolute sincerity, and it did not anger me that she was so sincere, but that her sincerity was without restraint and her grief so animal.

Sarah Bernhardt was nothing but declamation and pose.

Duse was everything. She was too many things all together; she was too fascinating, and when you roused yourself from the fascination you felt sick, as though you had drunk heavy wine.

Hamlet is unplayable. It is pure psychology carried onto the stage, and it never becomes action. None of the great Shakespearian tragedies lend themselves to being played. Only Othello, impersonated by Salvini, who was a sort of intellectual ox. He understood nothing, he didn't enter at all into the character, but he made an epic out of it with the sound of the words.

Diderot is more and better than an eighteenth century man because he immediately touches on human interests and situations. When one speaks of eighteenth century rationalism one forgets that rationalism may be found in all centuries. But the eighteenth century put all of its ardor into rationalism. It was the renaissance of science: there was for physics the same passionate ardor that there had been for Greek discoveries in the fifteenth century.

January 4, 1933
   I have just been reading Racine and Shakespeare almost contemporaneously, and the only comparison I could find for the impression they have left on me would be this: Racine delineates his figures like an excellent Greek ceramicist of the sixth century. Shakespeare is Rembrandt in about 1650.

Two different worlds, each at its culmination. *Phèdre* is all music, with no storms.

January 5, 1933

Why tell about crimes? Today's tragedy should have no deaths. Let's leave the cadavers to Shakespeare, whose trage-dies cannot be played because either they become ridiculous or they make your hair stand on end with horror. Shakespeare torments me; Shakespeare needs a prose reduction; given three of his phrases, there will be one which is ununder-standable — I challenge any Englishman whatever to under-stand it — but the other two will transfigure you.

I hope that you untiring renovators of interior decoration and fashions are already touched by admiration for David. Following the vogue for Louis Philippe, David is having his hour. And I prophesy that the next favorite will be Domeni-chino. After Domenichino it is Raphael's turn, and the wheel has come full circle.

Crowe and Cavalcaselle[1] lavishly throw insipid adjectives into their criticism, the way Saint Francis sprinkled ashes from the sleeves of his habit onto well-cooked food which he was obliged to eat when he was invited to dine with lay people.

[1] Sir Joseph Archer Crowe and Giovanni Battista Cavalcaselle collabo-rated on *New History of Painting in Italy* (1864–71) and other works on art.

January 7, 1933

The coast from Hyères to Toulon could be a piece of Greek coast along the outskirts of Corinth — the Acrocorinth being the fortifications above Toulon. The city and its surroundings are no different (seen from above) from the inhabited areas of those times — perhaps a little more thickly settled. But there is antique peacefulness here too, with scarcely even an occasional line of smoke on the horizon, and even that could be the distant mists, because Toulon is not a center for either commerce or industry.

The line of coast, stretched out so along the sea, is less grandiose than the Greek and Sicilian coasts; it is more gently romantic, it is a complicated flourish, a froth, like the elaborately elegant signature of a Sultan.

January 11, 1933

Lawrence is an inhibited man who feels the menace and the fear of his own inhibition. This is why he cries out against the inhibitions of others: to find courage and to feel that he is strong; but this internal passion veils the light of his intelligence, which would be extremely strong otherwise. Blessed are the impotent who are resigned and satisfied.

Troilus and Cressida by Shakespeare does not seem a live work to me because of the vicissitudes of the sad love affairs which he relates, particularly, but because of its Homeric presentation — for the heroes and the times of Homer, like a series of great panels in which the simple and rich life of the ancients unfolds as the Renaissance saw it. It is altogether different from the elaborately elegant rhetoric of Racine.

January 12, 1933

Right from my youth I have been agitated by the problem of bearing witness (evidence) — that problem which is the pivot and the kernel of *The Brothers Karamazov*. Human minds do not recognize it in the same way, since judgment depends on men's momentary conditions, almost on their "climate," and while intelligence may unite them, passion makes them discordant. Dostoevsky is able to take everyone's part very strictly, and recognizes the human will and moral effort even of characters who should be odious; but they are not odious because on the whole they do whatever they know and can. Dostoevskian judges and policemen are not ugly and wicked, but are beings circumscribed by the machine which employs and twists them. And they exhaust themselves uselessly in the direction of error.

In *The Brothers Karamazov* everyone is right; and it is right that the crime be a mystery. This sense of the necessity of each act, of the necessity of doubt and of error, is something never before reached in literature; it is like a breath of interstellar space . . .

January 13, 1933

There is never any "squalor" in an Italian landscape, while in France the towns, suburbs, the isolated houses, fall from the picturesque into the squalid and are surrounded by untilled land, refuse, debris. The one thing which offends me in Italy is the pretense: the false new and the false old which one sees cropping up here and there in constructions and reconstructions. The natural instinct of Italians would be very simple; it is cultural superstructures which lead them to vault their sobriety and their innate sense of proportion.

Lawrence's poetry is direct, clear, spontaneous; the image is born of the idea, it is not dispersed, and it reveals the idea. But the young consider him simplistic and are all for Eliot. Eliot may have his ideas, many ideas, but the young love him because he confuses and hides them. I would like him to do in his poetry what he does in his prose — to express his ideas clearly and limpidly, to stop playing at blind man's buff.

Though much more terse than Whitman, Lawrence resembles him in some way in his poetry, but he does not achieve the magnificence of Whitman — the sonority of his diction. The longer poems are catalogues at times, and raw material. But in his epigrams he is all intelligence and acumen. Lawrence's case is parallel to that of Carlyle; like Carlyle, he believes himself to be a thinker and a prophet, while he is merely an artist.

January 15, 1933

Architecture is a function of structure; and that means the sense of the mass, of the weight, of the solidity, of what is stable. When they used to build with great dispensing of masses — with vast walls and relatively restrained apertures, that is, before certain technical capabilities had been reached,

as in the Romanesque era, the results were absolutely "architectonic" buildings — fully aesthetic models of architecture.

The most "full" architectural type is the Romanesque
church and perhaps the Roman aqueduct. Too many of the
Greco-Roman buildings are in ruins to know exactly how they
were. In ruins one can read anything; they are no longer
objective "types."

The Egyptian temples are ruined on the inside; we do not
know what they were like, and the exterior is disfigured by
the columns, whose capitals are beautiful but which rise
from a large round base, the contrary of the "ideal" column.
One might say that architecture, like every art, loses its vigor
with technical progress. Today one can make do with anything: houses made of paper. But how can one ever manage
to "make felt" the structure of a paper house? We have
arrived at this point: that the Soviets have realized this impossibility and have returned to a classical ideal — to an art
wherein one feels the pre-eminence of man over the machine.
Capitalist art, they say, "represents" the machine, and our art
must show man victorious. It is what I said was the meaning
of the art of the Renaissance. Renaissance palaces are façades,
frontispieces; inside there might not be anything. What was
it that inspired those artists? Roman monuments in minia-
ture, which to some extent still exist and which were still
intact at that time all over Rome. They are like stone drawings. Brunelleschi's cupola, with the drum, the apse, and the
chapels in a circle, seems to be inscribed in a great arc (it
has no relation to the nave) and fills that flat space; it makes
a beautiful effect but it gives no sense of depth.

With Michelangelo things change. The cornice and the

base give a sense of solidity to the façade of Palazzo Farnese; there is a weight to support and a structure which supports that weight. But Michelangelo destroys certain of the Renaissance schemes, anticipating the Baroque. The Baroque is a Gothic interpretation of Roman elements.

In truth the Baroque reassumes and re-elaborates the preceding styles, and returns to a search for effects of depth. The curves, and the effort to somehow centralize its constructions, are responses to this. It is new decoration made entirely of well-known elements; in many, even too many, cases it reached an excess of decoration by combining too many of these elements together. To me, Palladio is the consummate artist of the Baroque; he re-creates the unique structure of a building, with long pilasters which run the whole height to open the house and support the tympanum; he renounces the horizontal symmetry of the plain Renaissance style.

The material one adopts is one of the effects, one condition, but it is not really everything in architecture. The Pentelican marble of the Parthenon and the bricks and rocks of the temples at Agrigento are scarcely relevant with respect to the "form"; their location (position) is far more important. The Parthenon has everything: excellent material and location, and an aesthetic idea behind its construction. When the Parthenon was painted, the marble must have been translucent, and perhaps the zones of color made the verticality of the columns stand out in clear contrast to the movement of the pediment. In principle there is nothing to forbid the construction of a reinforced concrete, or steel Parthenon.

Cubism is the ostentation of the obvious. Everyone knows that in painting, as in architecture, one has to be able to feel the skeleton, the mass, that which exists underneath and inside; and everyone does feel this in a work of art, no matter how little they may realize it. The Cubists need to whet this sensibility by giving nothing but the skeleton, the mass, the structure, but in trying to prove too much, they lose their real objective.

Probably the late Gothic, bewitched by height, actually lost the sense of height by constructing very very thin glass houses — in the same way that the bamboo tree never gives us the same sense of soaring that a column does, no matter how high it rises.

Shakespeare's sonnets may well be partly by Sidney; those which are definitely Sidney's own are beautiful. The sonnet was a very closed form, not only rhythmically but also intellectually, insofar as the images, the locutions and the thought which were condensed therein were concerned; and everyone in the same generation used it.

January 19, 1933
Ojetti and Edith Wharton have this in common: that they don't want to take part in discussions. Ojetti because he is afraid of compromising himself, Mrs. Wharton because she is afraid of compromising herself and of being bored.

January 22, 1933
If someone doesn't hurry up and bury George Moore's pen in his tomb it will keep on writing, and the books which will

issue forth will be scarcely less good than those he wrote in life.

When Don Achille Ratti[1] was helping me research the books in the Ambrosian Library there was a light and a gleam in his eyes which I also saw in Wilson's eyes before he had become a public figure and was only a history professor at Princeton. I saw neither the Pope nor Wilson again after their ascent to power.

With the mechanical means which are at the disposal of tyrants today, tyrannies should endure indefinitely. They will endure until a spring breaks in the tyrant's heart, until he himself collapses and is enervated. This cannot fail to occur, since the soul of a tyrant is consumed by the tension and fear which tyranny inspires in him.

January 24, 1933

Mantegna is not a poet, but a prose writer like Walter Savage Landor (better than being like Flaubert); Bellini is truly a great poet.

Saint Paul interests us very much, but he is too intellectual, too impassioned, and too Jansenist to conquer our souls; instead, how close Saint Peter is to us, to all times and to all men! Saint Peter has the qualities of a dolt, a coward, a renegade, a materialist; he cuts a poor figure in front of a foolish woman; and yet precisely because of all this he is so

[1] Pope Pius XI.

human, so simple and persuasive. He is a coward, truly cowardly, even in the act of unsheathing his sword and cutting the ear off the soldier, because in that moment he is violent — he takes leave of his senses — and only cowards are violent in that way.

January 25, 1933

A certain harmony of sensations, of feelings, of reaction, of desires; this is what makes up morality. Without this one cannot live.

Lawrence seems to have spent his life putting his sex foremost, while we on the other hand have made such an effort to keep ours in order and bridle it.

The first pages of *Sea and Sardinia* polish off Garibaldi in twelve lines with more intelligence than we find in the three fat volumes by George Trevelyan. What a historian he could have been! He takes after Carlyle more than anyone — the Carlyle of the posthumous portraits, which Carlyle must have made use of in the publication of his *Cromwell*. Lawrence's other consummate faculty is for making vibrant the most futile moments of the day, like taking a train, or watching people go by. One could spend entire days reading his prose about these facts. Boredom takes over when he pontificates and intellectualizes — when he falls into his confused and engrossing obsession.

Where can one find the limits between wit, humor, and "cocasserie" ("drôlerie")? It is not true that there is "esprit" only in France and "humor" only in England; one can hardly notice the slight difference in the tendencies of the two countries. There are great men who lack "humor" in England too: Gladstone, Wordsworth. Lacking humor does not necessarily mean a person is stupid. The French are always moralists and they therefore intellectualize their humorous faculty to make it serve a purpose. So one has "esprit," which is a useful condiment, interested in certain ends, while "humor" is always mobile, is an end in itself, is pure disinterestedness. "Cocasserie," which is a complete overturning, is not a primitive and free attitude of the spirit either, since it consists of a charge of total destruction — in a demonstration on behalf of absurdity. It has an excessive cast, it presupposes an absolute criticism of life which nothing can resist.

Not even Desmond MacCarthy makes pure "humor"; he combines the "cocasse" absurdity of the Irish with German intellectualism (his mother is German).

January 26, 1933

Politicians are absolutely, typically those who "videunt meliora et probantur, sed peiora sequuntur." They denounce the evils which afflict humanity (protection, armaments) but they do nothing to alleviate them because they can never decide to make the first move. Why not? Because they are occupied and preoccupied with the moment, they see no farther than their noses. They are very timid. They are like the sick man who could not decide to have a surgical operation while there was still time for it to cure him. The best, the purest, behave this way. Then there are the others who obey their own restricted, particular interests, or else obey a really very dangerous mania for giving birth to events — a need for novelty.

George Moore's style does not come from anyone; perhaps he learned his verbal aptness from Pater, but his special quality is not the appropriateness of his words. There is a special rhythm in his phrases, something extremely flowing, limpid, which I do not know in any other writers, either English or foreign.

Nietzsche is a man of extraordinary culture and one of the greatest and clearest thinkers of the last century. His madness begins when he gives free rein to his logic; logic as an end in itself is a destructive and absurd force. He rebelled against history not because he had no historic sense, but because he was offended by the way in which history had come to be written.

The nineteenth century, though it may be the century which invented historical method and seems to have lived almost uniquely for history, is nevertheless the one which has written the most tendentious history. It believed too much in its own false objectivity, in the supremacy of its own ideals; it was liberalistic instead of liberal, and Pecksniffian. Writers of Macaulay's ilk are the most guilty of this tendency — Nietzsche quickly rebelled against it and is thus the forerunner of all future rebellions.

Nietzsche is great in all his separate extracts; in the letters, in the scattered thoughts. Each of his phrases is a world.

The *Paralipomeni* are a masterpiece. But he is very great in *The Origins of Tragedy* as well.

January 27, 1933

Fra Angelico is a great artist, and is the first interpreter of landscape — much greater than Filippo Lippi. It is too bad that his angelicalities should attract above all the admiration of sterile English people of both sexes.

August 10, 1933

The explanation of Michelangelo's "dramas," created expressly by the literary romanticism of recent critics, is very simple: in the course of a work he would get tired at a certain point, would exhaust his vein, would lose interest. He had no preordained plans and projects, but an impulse, and this often vanished in him before the work was finished — finished, that is, in our eyes, because for him, in terms of his own sincerity, it was finished in the exact moment that the inspiration ceased. Thus his sketches are not sketches but are fully concluded works; to have gone any farther would have been a falsified effort. And anyway, the "final touches" which please unimaginative minds are often false; they are like an interpolation, a fillip, or "love and kisses" . . .

Michelangelo had a broken back and was devoured by ambitions — of the kind we would call snobbish. His relationship with Vittoria Colonna, his sonnets, are often manifestations of this spirit in him. And running alongside these ambitions a great sordidness and avarice.

The climate of his culture is medieval and Dantesque; he

did not know Latin, and thus approached the ancient world as well as the Bible by way of Dante. The whole iconography of the *Last Judgment* is medieval.

Pederasty was the tormenting passion of his life. No great artist ever loved the youthful male as he did. But this has nothing to do with his art.

It is logical that the Rococo should make its appearance at Baalbec, as it does also in the rocks of Petra; form always develops according to a rule of its own, so long as no violent interruptions occur. This signal, having barely appeared in the Hellenistic world, which was doomed to extinction, would instead eventually triumph after the Renaissance, when it would be left free to unfold itself.

I don't mean to say that the individual artist does not count. It is he who gives the push, who takes form a milimeter, sometimes a decimeter ahead of the prescribed measure. One can even say that the individual is so important that he is fatal. A Michelangelo had to exist in Florence in those years (no matter what his name might have been). And this is the true artist's personality; if you look at our modern artists — eccentric, changeable, and almost "enigmatic" in each manifestation of their work, one sees that it is they and not ancient art which are impersonal.

Is mystical and medieval Latin a flower of corruption? If so, then in the same way the mosaics are corrupt. There is no difference in animating spirit between San Vitale in Ravenna and the first hymns of Christian poetry. ("Christian" is a term which should be ignored in art; Roman, Hellenistic, Byzantine make sense; though, were I ever to write, as I hope to, a book on late antiquity, I would never even adopt "Roman." There is no difference in the make of a pagan sarcophagus and a Christian one; if the symbolism is unclear one cannot decide to which religion the sarcophagus belonged. The profane mosaics have been destroyed, but they must have been innumerable, and they would not have been distinguishable from the mosaics in churches.)

To return to "corruption," to "decadence" — God knows if there are signs of pride, of cruelty, of wickedness, of equivocal awesomeness in the mosaics which we admire so much. The figures have nothing about them which is either sacred or peaceful; yet they are beautiful, with the same subtle, profound, and even equivocal beauty which animates the Latin of the hymns.

August 11, 1933

Communism lives in the minds of men only as a sort of picnic, as an ideal of youthful insouciance; when men seek stability they flee from communistic ideals. The hope of fundamental changes in human nature by way of social changes is so fallacious; it means reckoning without anthropology. The most anthropological institution of all is the Catholic Church; she leaves human nature as it is, combatting all the so-called "idealisms," and endures through time because she takes up the man who is left destitute and disillusioned after the momentary intoxication of his enthusiasms and his attempts at generosity.

It is the truth pure and simple that Wagner's art is decadent. Wagner is the glorifier of the fatal man, of the fatal woman, of the fatal passion. Sensuality taken in itself is a natural and healthy thing, and so is melancholy, but when sensuality and melancholy are allied to make a single body, then we have artistic expressions which instigate the morbid passions (if one is so disposed). Thus the last notes of *Die Walküre*.

For the common man the hero is not a man entirely different from himself, but is a multiplication of himself — one who commits actions easy or comprehensible for all, but excessively magnified. Lindbergh.

August 12, 1933

It is denied Americans to have any cultural interest without its becoming a fad. They do not know how to be historians without becoming fiercely partisan toward some one point in history, ignoring all the rest. The American medievalists are held by a macabre passion for the Middle Ages, by religious fanaticism, and they try to impose this twisted mentality of theirs on everyone.

If individual well-being was going to have to lead to the destruction of civilization through the form of Communism, I would prefer that the individuals perish rather than the civilization.

The Germans have given up profound thought for complicated thought, and adopt metaphysical jargon in treating of any subject whatsoever — the most practical as well as the most exacting. Complicating the obvious is really a waste of energy which my patience cannot endure.

August 13, 1933

Men will surely be reduced to working three hours a day. But how will they pass the rest of their time? People who are by nature uneducated for leisure and repose, who do not desire it and who do not know what to do with it, will have to be taught how to use it.

We are now paying the fief of the great illusion of the last century — the price of that abnormal practice by which we lived at the expense of the lesser nations, imposing a horde of products on them which our industry was producing en masse. This was the only way in which "prosperity" was obtained, but it was a real infatuation, which perforce had to exhaust itself. And this is the meaning of the crisis now.

Two shocks in my life have profoundly shaken me: when I learned that the dissolution of the atom was possible, and when I saw the disintegration and the dissolution of Germany. Even during the war, when I had become accustomed to the idea of catastrophes, I never imagined that in Europe a defeat could have such total and fatal consequences.

If adolescents are healthy they accept the world as it is, feeling themselves unhesitatingly at its center. So, precisely because they believe it to be as stable as a rock, they set out to agitate it, to stir it up; they have a taste for testing their strength without any fear of the consequences. Only at the age of forty did I realize that the world is as volatile as can be and that conditions which used to seem necessary to me are as elusive as smoke.

I have always maintained that a novelist's best inspiration is not that which comes directly and immediately from whatever happens to him, but is that which comes from narrated facts passing through the screen of another voice, because this way he can approach them with more freedom of imagination and less scruple as to their truth — less vital participation. This was the sort of inspiration Proust derived from his mentor, Montesquiou, and this was also Scott's. We know now precisely what Scott's sources were: various people in his family who told him long stories about recent but already bygone times.

August 14, 1933

Eliot is an excellent writer and thinker when he writes about generic things, about economics and politics, but he does not have any feeling for poetry; he considers every poetic enchantment purely sensual and negligible, and he stops short with the gnomic, wanting to throw light on that alone. Without his knowing it, there is a lively Puritan foundation in him as there is in all New England Americans who today are more apt to be anti-puritan Puritans. As for Eliot's poems, he certainly possesses ability and a sense of rhythm, a jazz rhythm. He also understands the morning after — that vague disgust for the thing possessed, known, learned, the vague nostalgia for innocence. But otherwise, in his poems, there is nothing but a vein of parody: he transplants former poetry in full awareness of what he is doing, and by transplanting it deforms it and makes it serve his own ends.

August 15, 1933

I recently tried to read *Salammbô*; it has the same effect on me as swallowing a ton of turtle soup. *Salammbô* has never seemed to me to be alive as a work, but more like a series of bas-reliefs; like a museum filled entirely with pieces of porphyry.

August 16, 1933

Michelangelo should have died at the age of forty, once the Sistine Chapel was finished. This way the *Last Judgment*, the tombs, the Pauline Chapel and some other things would have been lost, but on the other hand what would have been gained would be not having to reckon, now, with his overpowering influence having spread out everywhere. In Florence the direction of art was set by this time, but in other places the effects of the Michelangelesque example were deleterious. The rhetoric of muscle, of stress, of the enormous, of heroic sentiment, coming out in souls who were not born to be a part of all this, muddied the next artistic generation everywhere; from the Carracci to Titian and to Tintoretto, and even to the late Raphael, without counting the foreigners. When human energy is this powerful it is devastating; think of Wagner.

August 17, 1933

Men do not desire happiness, men desire to live; they aspire to a certain violence of sensations, to a mixture of grief and well-being, and for the sake of this they will forfeit the peace of their souls with no remorse.

August 18, 1933

Coleridge had within himself the raw material, the potentiality, of a Goethe, but he did not have an "Olympian" physique. His opium addiction is none other than the indication of the weakness which kept him from fully realizing his own qualities.

August 24, 1933

Order is an instinct which manifests itself in children and is already present in animals; it is a powerful instinct because it conserves and saves human strengths. Man normally flees from anarchy because it costs him too much energy and devastates, so to speak, his spirit. The instinct for knowledge is by nature anarchic; if it is not regulated it can be destructive. For this reason timid people and people interested in some given order fear it and hinder it.

The field, or rather the fields, of knowledge are incredibly vast. One thinks of how much daily effort is given rise to by specialized technical development, even down to the manias and fads which little by little find ways of organizing themselves and which are pure curiosity and badly directed, or rudimentary, "knowledge." There are territories of whose confines we are not even aware, and branches of knowledge whose origins and direction we do not know at all. Our knowledge circles around one point of view; whatever lies outside our angle of vision disappears, or in a pale, unfocused manner only appears to our mind at certain times. Mental modes depend on changes in the visual ray; something which at first escaped us fixes itself in our center of vision and predominates in the world's eye for a more or less extended period of time. Then other objects of the mind which had been on the periphery pass in full fire and occupy everyone's attention while the first vanish. Anyone whose mind is wide awake and who seeks vaster comprehension does feel the presence of these things belonging to the past and to the future; he is aware that there will be changes in the problems which seem the most universal; but it is like a remote sense which lies at the margin of reality, a pale presentiment of the future.

August 26, 1933

What have I done in my whole life? Nothing which has any more importance than that piece of grass which you are picking. I was born for sensual contemplation. I mean exactly that: sensual, voluptuous; not for mathematical contemplation. Not even in my early years, when the desire to express myself was most urgent, did I ever have to place work in the first rank. And like the Indian sages, I ought to have retired at the age of forty to another life, a life of communication with nature, and of solitude; of contemplating natural spectacles with no thoughts. Now however I am kept busy with little problems whose solution will not be of any use to anyone, or will be useful to those few people who do feel compelled to proceed along my narrow path. No, the labor of a writer is not justifiable without the creative faculty; only poetry counts, or such prose as corresponds to imaginative creation. For the diffusion of ideas the word is sufficient.

I should have been born into the favorable society of the eighteenth century, when it was sufficient to converse, when classicism and humanism had become refined and aired, and the stability of political institutions could be placed in doubt; when people amused themselves with the most diverse thoughts, and paradox was born — that is, the other face of Truth was discovered. I mean the French eighteenth century; England at that time was still archaic and socially hidebound, as is illustrated on the one hand by Doctor Johnson and on the other by Horace Walpole, who, despite his intellect, conducted himself in a worldly manner and frequented worldly circles exclusively.

The greatest English prose writer is Arnold; before him it was Addison, and since his death there has been nobody. His prose is a simple medium like pure water. His poetic instinct found expression in verses which are the most beautiful English verses since Wordsworth, so for this reason his prose is free of any residue and is clearly expository. Walter Pater, on the other hand, believes in "artistic" prose; his prose is irrigated by his poetic vein which has no other outlet; and you cannot manage prolonged consumption of his prose — it is food which is too rich and too delicious.

August 27, 1933

Phariseeism attaches itself parasitically to anyone who considers himself the custodian of truth.

You need to be adolescent to make pronouncements about the why and the wherefore of things; later on one realizes that things *are,* simply, and then any critical explanation, any inquiry whatever as to their nature, appears to be just one more useless attempt. One can, with maturity, acquire a sure eye and give an exact judgment as to how things "stand," but this judgment is of no interest to the young. The young want a message, they want excitement, and they easily find this in dishonest authors with few scruples, who do not know the limits of their own minds and who are seeking applause in anything they do.

I wrote to an American friend of mine about what seems to me to be my position in Michelangelesque criticism. I constructed with my own hands a sort of viaduct or tunnel which put me in communication with Michelangelo, then the Germans came and defecated copiously in it, so that now the road which once was open to me is almost impossible to traverse because of the stink. The Germans surrendered themselves, with all their confused energies, with all their metaphysical passion, to the "problem" of Michelangelo and Leonardo, but more to Michelangelo. They are attracted by the titanic, the violent, the almost monstrous elements which they can find in him. There is something fundamentally violent and barbaric in the German spirit, as though they were three centuries behind the rest of the civilized world.

August 28, 1933

Rockefeller is like Michelangelo in having been the exponent of a given situation; he was the one who channeled and represented certain forces, certain needs which had to have been expressed and which found their "type" in him. Rockefeller is synonymous with a certain sense of profiteering, a special spirit of initiative and coordination which has something gigantic and majestic about it, totally unscrupulous and almost bloated in its substance. In another sense his case is parallel to that of the "capitalists" of the Middle Ages. Like them, his conscience pushes him to make people forget the wealth he has accumulated, and in the same way that they founded monasteries and colleges, he devotes himself, with the same spirit of expiation, to the founding of institutions of all sorts. It bodes ill that today (or yesterday) his architecture is not uniformly good architecture. Even in the old days not everything about the foundations was excellent, but their particular challenge to the centuries did lie in their architectonic solidity, and then as the centuries have gone by they have known better days. Perhaps the Rockefeller institutions will also live through a better time than this, which is so marked by philanthropic unctuousness.

Landscape in painting today demonstrates to me that the most refined, most purified sense of color comes when it tends toward monochrome. Three years or so ago I took a great many notes on "color" (which so many people accused me of not taking into consideration in my studies). I ought to be able to use them as a new chapter to be added to my essays on the Renaissance painters.

I know very little, and know it badly, about people's characters, which is what gives rise to suspicion in me. It's not that I have a suspicious nature; it is the fruit of my ingenuousness and of my candor. It is the sense that everyone knows how to deceive me by entering my good graces, and can then profit from it.

August 29, 1933

Croce (*Poesia Popolare e Poesia d'Arte*) cares too little about the other arts to investigate the most interesting problem connected with Michelangelo's poetry, which is that one should study whether the sonnet form in that specific period — at the point to which it had been brought by the Petrarchans — was such that it could permit (as sculpture permitted it) the expression of the roughness and asperity which underlies Michelangelo's soul and that is not a form of coarseness on his part, or a proof of ignorance, but expresses the essential element of his art. Literarily, Michelangelo was far from ignorant; he was nurtured on Petrarch, had lived in the echo of Poliziano and the Medici, and he had been possessed by enthusiasm for poetry since his youth. The sonnets come out of his later years; but so also do his least finished sculptures: from the many Pietàs to the group in Palestrina, if it is his. And thus in the sculpture one sees the same roughness as in the poetry; it is not the writer's unskillfulness which is responsible for their being hard, even unsatisfactory. I am asking questions, I am not expounding conclusions, and I would like other people, who have a more genuine sense of Italian literature than I do, to respond.

Napoleon lacked opportunities; Fate took hold of him right from the start and led him to disaster. So one can say very little about him, about his greatness. About Napoleon III one can say that his destiny was like a post-hypnotic phenomenon, dominated by the sign and the fortunes of Napoleon the Great, and by his own attempts to justify himself: a dream life, which did tend toward realizing something of what Napoleon, on Saint Helena, had wanted to demonstrate as having been his task and his mission. Thus the mind of Napoleon III was subjugated by the idea of Italy's unification. When he became afraid of his phantom he lost his own genuineness and the rest of his imperial career from '60 on is pitiful.

Medieval theology is more human and more complete than Bolshevik theology, and by medieval theology I mean both that complex of norms and beliefs which inspired the political thought of that time, and the Church. The barbarity of the Middle Ages is indicated only by the terrible conditions of life, which were far worse than those in Russia, but the feudal system was able to conquer and ameliorate these conditions in a marvelous way, because it was shot through with fruitful civil thinking. Marxist thought is extremely limited — barely a slender canal running between iron banks. If conditions in Russia were to improve, and nothing would give me greater happiness, there would always be this constriction, this habit of a closed theology with no way out — which would never allow freedom of thought even to the person enjoying the greatest wealth of opportunity. The regimes of the past have all agitated on behalf of becoming civilized because the inspiration behind them was better founded, and they consolidated in history in proportion to the good, or to the least evil, which they were able to produce. They only fell when they had reached the inertia of old age. With Bolshevism people want to establish the dominion of logic, but are forgetting that man is anthropological. What response will future years give to this error?

August 30, 1933
    There comes a moment of perfect liberty in adolescence, when a boy is liberated from the chains of maternal love and does not yet know those of romantic love. It is a moment of complete disinterestedness, of complete clairvoyance, which will never be found in life again.

    Any great organism whatever loses its mobility and becomes stagnant when it becomes hypertrophic. In the nineteenth century the bourgeoisie gave rise to concentrations of industry which have since shown this tendency to blow themselves up and paralyze themselves; and as demands and needs have grown, the state too now tends to supplant industrial activity with an even vaster and more centralized organism, and it too is headed for paralysis. The perfect balance would be the concurrence and concomitance of medium-sized organisms, impelled by individual interests —

economic and scientific interests — which might guarantee and permit freedom for new combinations around it, even at the cost of a certain amount of waste. Waste is the other face of experimentation. The Ptolemaic kingdom was a centralized and equalitarian state, and what were its consequences, if not to have taken from its people their spontaneous resources, the very vitality which would have permitted it to defend itself? Thus it fell to the first invasion by the Moslem people.

Individual genius leads, in the scientific field, to research and to the discoveries which then transform themselves into prosperity; but how does this genius manifest itself? By pure chance? No — only in those places where life is rich and full, in tune with civilization. It is like the highest froth on the highest wave.

Landed property had a function and a hereditary meaning in the state in times when, because of difficulties of communication, the central power had to find stable agents in its territories, whose tasks were those of delegated sovereignty. But once conditions changed it is right that the rules governing this property should have changed, that its indivisibility and the rights of primogeniture should have ceased. It thus became simply personal property and there was no longer any sign of power connected with it.

October 17, 1933

Chateaubriand is a consummate rhetorician. He is continually accompanied by the roar of his prose, which acts as the tone and the orchestration of his sentiments. They are sentiments which he does not feel, or rather it is unimportant whether he feels them or not, but with lavish display he presents them and shows them off to others. This was the birth of romanticism; he, a man of the eighteenth century, helped in its gestation. He was a great "inventor" and went about it in what could be called almost a classicizing manner. He knew nothing about America, he stayed the whole time in Philadelphia, and yet he was the first person to create the poetry of the American race and landscape.

It was only during the triumph of romanticism, much later therefore, that the exigencies of "true" and "lived" sentiments were born, when the writer's own experience was poured off still hot into his writings, and this is part of the fallacy of that era. In order to write, distance is necessary, and a screen which isolates and removes you from reality; this has been the office of mythology for so many centuries.

Duse suffered during her life; but she would have suffered much more from not suffering.

October 18, 1933

Chateaubriand is the prince of monochords. He was D'Annunzio's master in the art of living, but his was a much vaster field of life than D'Annunzio's — he had much more background, a much broader base, and many more roots. So the influence which he aroused was much more enduring and more profound — less vulgar.

October 19, 1933

Chateaubriand, says Lemaitre, has piety without having faith. We all share the same condition. The sense of "pietas" involved in religious acts is not only an aesthetic participation in the rite, it is a sense of respect for history; it is that ancient veneration which is still alive in us and to which we abandon ourselves with love.

The true rationalist generation is not mine but my father's; he had the enthusiasm and the courage of his own convictions, but we don't. Ever since we were young, and increasingly more so as we have grown old, we have been open to other voices besides that of strict reason. We have been open to all voices (or at least so we have thought) and we have been prepared to recognize the value and "novelty" of even the youngest; but these young ones — and I was thinking this yesterday evening when I was remembering Stefanik — have often turned to an enthusiasm of another kind — to mysticism — to forms of warmth and faith which we may see and understand but in which we cannot participate; and in relation to them we remain as exiles.

The Germans exaggerate their clothing. They camouflage and disguise themselves for every occasion, wearing the gaudy uniforms of their occupations, no matter how temporary (look at these tourists all decked out as if they were about to scale the most arduous peak) because they have a "horror vacui" of themselves.

October 21, 1933

William James took Papini seriously; being a philosopher he did not have a very exacting understanding of human values, and whoever addressed himself to him seemed to him to be gifted beyond a doubt with a thousand fine qualities. He was like a friend of mine, whom I had reproached for the predilection he showed for some dreadful man, and who answered: "Que voulez-vous que je ne l'aime pas, puisqu'il m'adore." [1]

The knights errant were simply the youngest sons in feudal families, who had neither a position nor a stable occupation within the castle. Then when the time came that they were not satisfied with individual adventures, they formed coalitions and the "expeditions" were born — first in Spain against the Arabs, then the crusades in the Holy Land, and finally the Teutonic Order's "colonization" along the edges of the Baltic. But it was a colonization without colonists. These youngest sons landed on infidel lands and then burghers and Jews followed after them to found the cities; right up to the present day the only natives are the peasants.

October 23, 1933

Writers, with their love of the words and usages peculiar to their own mannerisms, often go so far in that direction that they exhaust their own language. I call this phenomenon private language. It is like an enclosure into which others are forbidden to penetrate. The tone of Swinburne's poetry is of this nature, and we have the greatest and most typical example in the work of Rabelais. D'Annunzio's sin is not in his creating a sacred domain of this kind for himself, but in his lack of respect for the confines of others.

1 "How can you expect me not to like him when he adores me?"

October 24, 1933

The history of Greece takes us step by step in the wake of a quarrelsome, inconclusive, resentful, spiteful, petty people. But they are the same people who were the custodians of humanity's highest ideals and who made manifest the greatness of art. And these two disparate factors go together much more than one would think.

When I was young there was a rich American engineer by the name of Horn who never used to sleep more than three hours a night and spent the rest of the time drawing — drawings which fell far below even a mediocre level. One evening, after giving dinner to several guests, Horn brought out an enormous portfolio to which he had consigned the best of his output. The portfolio passed from hand to hand among his guests; all of us looked through the drawings and remained in glacial silence. Only the painter La Farge (who was already quite well known), being the last to open it, finally said: "My dear Horn, I am terribly sorry, but the light here is mediocre and also I am tired out from a long day's work; I really cannot say anything. Let me take the portfolio away; tomorrow I will look at it by the light of day." I was stunned to hear such a neatly jesuitical discourse, in which any outright lie was avoided, and I said to myself — how incompetent I am; what a clod, a boor, a newborn babe who knows absolutely nothing about dealing with people or extracting myself from messy situations.

Lord Strathcona, a young Scotsman stationed in Montreal during the early years of the English occupation of Canada, was extremely handsome and had no sooner arrived than he began to be rather too attractive to the wife of the governor of the Hudson's Bay Company, which at that point ruled the fate of the colony. So after a few months he was sent, as though exiled, to the port on Hudson's Bay where he stayed for several years, the only Englishman among the Esquimos. A sail only put in there once a year. But Lord Strathcona imposed on himself and maintained the self-discipline of dressing for dinner every evening, and every morning of pressing and opening up the copy of the *Times* of the corresponding day in the preceding year, thus putting himself in step not with time, but with the sun.

Oscar Wilde, having very clearly failed to meet some commitment, telegraphed: "I cannot come. Lie follows."

October 25, 1933

From the cradle to the tomb I have been and will always be a fervent follower and champion of intelligence. But intelligence alone, in its gaseous state, without the ballast of experience, plays ugly jokes. Keynes' case is a typical example: he knows nothing about financial practice, and is disturbing the world with his very intelligent and very absurd theories.

Only one thing is more boring than a showy display of vice; a continual search for novelty.

October 26, 1933

Tennyson took everything from Keats, but he is like Keats drawn out and sweetened.

To me the ideal Italian prose is Leonardo's prose: it is their only prose which is exempt from an infatuation with Cicero.

The Italians do wrong to be dressed by Prandoni; he could only dress one tenth of the aristocratic types well — that one tenth which possessed Apollonian beauty. They are dressed by Prandoni, they speak in Prandoni's terms, and publish books in Prandonian editions. They always favor too shiny a surface, a suit which is a mannikin and is the contrary of form. Form should be structure, should arise entirely from internal exigency. When the aspects of appearance are so underlined and obvious, then what seems to be form makes everything detached and is empty.

October 27, 1933

Lawrence is a Carlyle for adolescents.

Moravia sees everything as black, and needs rain as the background for his action, but this is because things present themselves to him and are formed in this way in his mind, it is not because of any urgency or moral concept; it is because of his own conscious will for pessimism, and this has nothing to do with artistic creativity. If writers today only appreci-ate the most lugubrious aspects of reality, the most pessimistic naturalism, it is because their images are formed this way spontaneously, because they are children of their time, and our time is very unstable. It is the reaction to the nineteenth century, which was a great century of faith, faith in one's own forces and one's own values, if not in the ancient myths. Today there is only faith in the scientific myths — not truths, but certainly substantial myths — but the faith is so widespread that we are not even able to think of them as myths. The ideal for the mature man is to have overcome his faith in myths, but to stay open to faith in the eventual truth which intelligence may discover; but there are very few mature men. Most people remain intellectually or spiritually infantile — perpetual twelve- or thirteen-year-olds; some pass the age of puberty and are then eternal adolescents, which makes them extremely fascinating. It is also easier to "mature" in eras during which faith is inevitable (like the middle of the nineteenth century, or the middle of the thirteenth century), when the general usage and consumption of a type of belief helps and promotes whatever manifestations of vitality there may be.

In all of Pirandello, and especially in his works for the theatre, there is something too constructed; when you look closely there is a mechanism — one which is not psychological but ideological.

If the colors with which the great painters of the Renaissance painted were to come to light once again we would scream; there is no more inflamed palette than Titian's as his contemporaries saw it. The "tone" of the old masters is given by the layers of dust, of grease, of almost human sweat, in which the centuries have clothed them, and by now the eye is so accustomed to this surface that any cleaning or return to the original conditions astounds and enrages the so-called knowledgeable public.

A love for somber tones, for black and white, was born with neoclassicism; what came then in reaction to the eighteenth century's pleasant decorative style was a renewal of inspiration from classical monuments, and since these had been reduced to nakedness through the years (whereas in Roman times not one square centimeter had been without color) they affirmed that tendency toward the severity of neutral, pallid colors. Yet, in the best neoclassicists, in David and Ingres, there is color, and it counts a great deal.

In all events, I can make no distinction between design and color, except the distinction which goes no farther than the purely technical process; one draws with charcoal, or a burin, or with color. One speaks of "colorists" to indicate a particular function of color, a special scheme; but all the great painters are colorists, and they all know how to draw.

Art should not be taught in schools, but in workshops, right there with the painters. Art is a trade; and it is from the trade, properly learned, that in good time artistic creation can be released.

November 7, 1933

The dilettante is someone who cannot put up with boredom. Any work whatever involves moments of the most funereal boredom which one must have the strength to overcome in order to then reach the happiness of a result. The dilettante is unable to do this — so he never gets any farther than the fragment, the crumb — he lacks any ties between the subjects of his delight, so his delight results as whim rather than an experience. Dilettantes do not follow any regular path, but leap from one thing to the other, like flamingoes in a swamp.

Khalepà tà kalà:[1] three Greek words which I learned in my early youth. Because the dilettante does not undergo the labor of difficulty he also loses the whole meaning of beautiful things. He stands poised on the peaks as though he had arrived there by airplane, and does not know that in order to enjoy the glory of them he has to have come to know the whole massive mountain step by step.

November 9, 1933

Laclos already contains all of Stendhal, except Cherubino's aria. Tonight I finished rereading *Les Liaisons Dangereuses*, which I had not reopened since I first read it at Harvard. I took it up again because of the need I feel to realign myself with the classics; this seems to me to be the only way of continuing my education into my last years.

The eroticism of Laclos is anything but sensual (and romantic sensuality is in fact the negation of eroticism), but it is not sadistic, since Laclos' cruelty has nothing to do with physical suffering; and it has nothing really to do with love. It is all a desire to dominate, to overcome the weaker, and to find satisfaction in the triumph of private vanity.

1 "The beautiful things are difficult" — a proverb attributed to Solon.

The impression, the feeling of things, which we want to describe is like a radiating chaos, but any description we make of it forms a tiny solid body which we labor to construct and which seems very poor and limited indeed. Then, through the irradiation of this internal chaos of ours, we realize that the tiny solid contains a great evocative power.

Thus I realize that the instrument with which we are endowed is always the same — the same at the age of twenty-five as it is at seventy. And this makes me sad. But this is why knowledge is necessary. The more we know, the more we open up the field in which our instrument can work. Thus at twenty-five I was able to be more direct and more lyrical in my letters, but now in anything I write my orchestration is richer, and this is all the effect of culture. The same thing has happened to greater men; the instrument, left to itself, has either become rigid or, sometimes, inflated and rhetorical. It would have been better if Michelangelo had died once the Sistine Chapel ceiling was finished; after that there is a tumescence in his work — a sort of brutal emphasis, an athleticism, which today (without knowing it) Mussolini is copying. Raphael is guilty of the same sort of brutality in the lower part of the *Transfiguration* (which is certainly his); before he died he had already become Giulio Romano. The Venetians were not this way; they matured and improved right on into their extreme old age. The motifs and types which the artists prefer are always the same, and constitute their instrument. When they limit themselves to the human figure, as the Florentines did, their repertoire quickly becomes stagnant. But the Venetians bathe the human figure in atmosphere and arrange it in landscape, so their work becomes complex and orchestrated; there is more fluidity to their compositions and to their colors, which tend toward a rich monochrome, merging with one another and bringing each other to life, while the Florentines tend toward an acid and detached polychrome. Andrea del Sarto is a Florentine who deserved to have become Giorgionesque, but how held back he was by his prejudice for the single human figure! Even he, by isolating it, lost its native grace; even his work reveals brutal insistence, an exaggeration of stylistic detail, a tendency toward heroic imposture. Many of the Venetian figures are also heroic in a certain sense, but they are always fused into and proportionate to the landscape.

November 11, 1933

There are moments in history in which everything is fused, plastic, malleable; and in these moments only a little push is needed in order to change the course of events. This push can come from an individual, but the individual who is capable of giving the push will himself be the best product of his time; he will hardly be differentiated from it as much as a fleck of foam on a huge wave.

The nineteenth century hit upon historical method, but the famous historians of the century did not know how to use it. It was a century of faith, and anyone who has faith in his own time cannot understand past times. The best historians are those who even in their dreams do not imagine that the best of all possible ages is the age in which they are living.

November 13, 1933

History should not be so much an account of facts as an account of illusions, because men act according to their illusions, and myths, much more than on the guidance of facts.

November 14, 1933

What I mean by "actualistic" drawing is drawing which has been done in such a way as to purposely reproduce the lines which would appear to the eye of the camera. However, none of the past masters could have this ideal, and the qualification of "realists" given them by the "actualists" of today is very badly chosen. We Nordics find there is something very closely related to our feeling in the drawing of the ancient Germans or Flemish, so we say, for example, that Holbein is a realist, but in fact he is not an "actualist" any more than Botticelli is, or the very abstract Antonello da Messina. All of these artists — equally and unconsciously — developed drawing which followed a certain scheme of their own, and Holbein's is one of the most geometrical — as geometrical, as I have said, as that of Antonello.

November 16, 1933

What is lacking in our age which is so intellectual is some measure and harmony of intellect — that "volupté" evoked by La Fontaine, which brings man back in touch with meaning, with reality. Nowadays man is reducing himself to a pure mental process, and by dint of abstractions, a terrible and cruel world is being formed.

November 19, 1933

It is true that creative artists experience difficult moments before reaching clarity of expression — moments of congestion and of grievous labor; but we critics are subjected to another torment, to the torment of ponderation and of judgment. Debating with myself over every single attribution without ever being sure of it gives me a great deal of pain and teaches me great humility.

The great majority of art critics are people who adopt a different jargon from mine to expound ideas which once were mine but which I discarded years ago.

November 20, 1933

Only idiots learn from experience, since wise men know about everything before undergoing it.

So often modern music is nothing but aural flagellation.

November 27, 1933

Mephistopheles has always been attractive to men because he is a figure who is comprehensible to them, pervaded with passion and rebellion, whereas God, the God of the Jews and the Christians, the God of Plato, is an inconceivable concept for most people; they can chew over the name almost like a magic formula, but without giving it any semblance of reality. By the same token artists have found it easy to represent Mephistopheles and to render him familiar and beloved because men recognize themselves in him and this is really what art consists of: rendering the states and moments of the human soul objectively, so that for anyone perceiving the art they may then become subjective.

The human mind always turns on the same subjects (the subjects "of the day" in the broadest sense) not because its sphere is restricted but because it implicitly has made a choice and does not perceive interests beyond certain predilected terms. Thus one cannot say that today "everything" is discussed; certainly certain things are discussed about which formerly no mention was made, but then no mention is made of others which once were predominant. All subjects are contemporaneously accessible to the best minds, but if they were all truly pursued there would be tremendous confusion; it is the choice and the limitations which constitute an order. Common minds are not aware of this limit, and believe in good faith that there are no possible subjects beyond those they hear everyday.

November 28, 1933

Every now and then I am assailed by a doubt: does man perhaps need war the way he needs religion? Every day we see that when the set forms of religion are denied, men invest the most absurd and harmful beliefs with a religious spirit, and thus we are convinced that everything must be done to protect and support the Church. Perhaps equally harmful and mortifying results would be reached if men were denied the possibility of war. Perhaps the meekness and docility of a whole race — like the Armenians and the Jews — which leaves such traces of cowardice and fear in their characters, comes precisely from their being so little used to war, or from their heightened sense of the injustice of armed violence. And so, for the real good of humanity, shouldn't we perhaps desire the perpetuation of the warrior spirit? Should we stop hoping for peace?

November 29, 1933

There would be no history of philosophy if the first philosopher had been understood by the second. All philosophers have rediscussed the problems because they have not understood the preceding solutions; because, that is, they have not understood one another.

November 30, 1933

Americans want to convert every country to their plumbing, and by that they think they are converting them to culture.

December 1, 1933

Makart, Lenbach, Lavery, Sargent, Laszlo, the fashionable painters of yesterday, are a band of "wish fulfillment" painters who flatter their clients instead of painting their portraits; who represent them "ideally" according to an ideal which falls between that of the hairdresser and the fashion store. Their parallel in sculpture is Canonica. No, Lenbach

is no better than the others, but perhaps he is more of a mys-
tifier; instead of a banal chic he tends toward a mysterious,
elevated chic, to a vulgar refinement. The society which
Lenbach painted was that which gave such enthusiastic and
exalted acclaim to the young D'Annunzio.

A clear thought is a maimed thought, expressed either by
an idiot or by a dishonest person — except in mathematics
where clarity is inherent in the postulates. The heroes of
clarity are the French, and they are the great planers-down
of reality. Translations into French are always perspica-
cious, but if you compare them with the text you see what
they have done: they have planed down all the sharp edges
and have avoided all the snags; so that it becomes like the
projection, rather than the representation, of a relief.

Perforce there are limits in me, in my mind and in my
character; if not I would not exist. Limitation is the condition of existence; thus God, who is limitless, cannot exist.

December 4, 1933

Spengler adopts the term "Catilinism" to denote any instance of base demagoguery, adulation of the proletariat; I
had already used the term more than forty years ago. It is a
phenomenon which is always restated, and can be embodied
in the person of Catiline because he is a historically conspic-
uous figure; but it developed above all in the Anglo-Saxon
countries during the course of the last century. It reaches a
point of the most abject servility to the man of the masses —

"oclolatria" [1] — and it produces an abasement of all the freedoms, because the proletarian mass does not know what it means to desire them.

Americans study art as though it were a matter of browsing through an herbarium, with the zest of a botanist who knows nothing about plants unless they are desiccated and crushed.

Alma-Tadema paints a Greece whose marble temples are like sections of sugarloaf overlooking a sea such as we find only in the most Mediterranean countries, and on days when it looks like a great basin of concentrated Prussian blue.

There is progress (I would rather not call it progress, I would rather define it with some less easy term) and it consists in the fact that there are more people today who are cognizant of high ideals. Even the vituperation against the present age, against its materialism, its lack of faith and its cruelty, is a sign of progress. We are becoming more and more indignant about the way things are. I, for example, who am not by nature a candid person, have never expected that people wanted to cheat me; if I had been born several centuries earlier I could have done no less than expect it, and form my own theory and practice of life accordingly. Besides, history is a reckoning of the stages through which man passes in his attempt to humanize himself; "ever more human" could be the motto of the ideal life of a man.

[1] In Greek: love of the mob.

December 9, 1933

Error is the most fruitful thing in the world, but given that it bears its fruit, it must immediately disappear.

March 10, 1934

"Vox, praeterea nihil": we are badly disappointed when one of the most famous and lavish autobiographies of all time reveals itself as being completely devoid of internal life. An extremely knowledgeable modulation of the voice; this is all Chateaubriand amounts to — this is the way women used to see him, leaning against the mantelpiece, without any real beauty, without any other source of fascination; and we hear the same voice in his memoirs — warm, beautiful, orchestral.

Architecture of surfaces, architecture of screens — this is the architecture of today; not buildings founded, planted in the earth, but poised on the soil as though they had been "mounted" somewhere on high and then a hand had deposited them on a table. It is the outcome of that frenzy for simplification that has possessed people's spirits from the war on — or even some years before; through which builders have fallen out of love with words (the columns, the arches) and have restricted themselves to using only syllables, this being the "new realism" and "rationality."

March 13, 1934

Turner is a man of genius, but a bad painter.

The aim of a novel is to bring firmly defined and meaningful characters to life: characters who acquire a force which goes beyond the pages of the book, and who reach the level of myths. Thus the "characters" move ahead by themselves; it is not important that they be recounted in detail and propelled by extraordinary happenings. The way in which the novel unfolds, whether it be biographical or analytical, whether it have a fast or a slow pace, is a secondary and "instrumental" question; new "instruments" are created gradually by the narrative; they are taken up, exploited and then thrown into a corner. These instruments are comparable to cinematography and photography with respect to the visual arts, but similarly they neither exhaust nor renovate "ab imo" the field of art. They are an outcome of fashion, and fashion continually varies and has good reason to vary. The importance of the creation of characters lies in presenting a life through them which is more strong and real than life itself; hence the myth. And when the figures have become transcendent as myths their specific precision is undone; their outlines then become vague and their fullness is such that we can ascribe all our desires and all our dreams to them.

We are bubbles of the earth[1] like the plants, like the animals, heated by the same sun. This pleases me: mother earth is my mother, not in an allusive sense, but in a fully real sense, while infinity, power, the divinity of human forces, are rhetorical words, evanescent forms of thought. I like Goethe's warning that man must above all be conscious of

[1] Paraphrased from Shakespeare, *Macbeth*, Act I, scene iii: "The earth hath bubbles as the water has/ And these are of them. Whither are they vanish'd?" and refers to the sudden apparition and sudden departure of the witches.

his limitations. We are birds tied to our cages with a string: farther than that we cannot fly. And how much genius it takes to fly all ten centimeters of its length!

The gadfly of my early youth was my compulsion to discover the meaning, the essence, of literature. No critic, no philosopher, no writer gave me the explanation I was seeking, and then suddenly in a flash I realized that to find it I would have to turn to the visual arts, so I set out on that path and am there still. But I am not forgetting, I have never forgotten, that it was a way which I took originally for a different purpose; and fragmentary notes which I have taken on my conclusions along more general lines can be published after my life has ended. I would like to work more, but I do not have enough energy. Whatever is left to me I must spend in the long work which I have set myself.

It is not true that there was a "break," in the nineteenth century, in the passage from classical art to impressionism. Impressionism is classical — more classical than the exaggerated, rigid, formal, boring neoclassicism which it succeeded. The eighteenth century experienced a graceful and frivolous classicism, but only in that external decoration, in scenery, which is called Rococo. The reaction, neoclassicism, was manifested by a return to seriousness, but it went too far, and the next upheaval brought art back to its origins, to a much more spontaneous and effective classicism. Impressionism is classical insofar as it directly achieves the end which every artist always puts to himself: to give a representation of reality which is altogether life-giving. The ideas of pantheistic immersion of man in nature are all philosophers' concepts, stuck on later. The painter wanted to paint, and succeeded in painting with a relatively new vocabulary and technique (the predominant use of landscape dates from much earlier) seeking to realize his intention by roads which had not yet been thoroughly traversed. One can say that he sought to give, on canvas, the momentary impression of color and light. So it is not a kind of painting which detached itself from man, which abandoned man; on the contrary, it turned to the life of the individual, and to his way of meaning and seeing. But neither, on the other hand, was it an arbitrary abolition of reality, since it took the visual realities: spectacle, "landscape," intensively into account. So there was no pause in the nineteenth century, and the history of art continues. There was a break, but it came much later on, around 1910, or with the war.

Raphael made more headway in twenty years of activity than Titian did in seventy; from the Perugino-like simplicity of the first works he arrived at the full Baroque of his *Transfiguration*.

March 14, 1934

Since the time living literatures have become material for university instruction, and, so to speak, classical — from the time of that affirmation of romanticism which encouraged and rekindled nationalism in so many different countries, — they have been "philologized" to an absurd degree; they used to present too little difficulty so that there was little occasion for pedantry in the study of them, whereas the dead languages are "ennobled" by the continual labor which one must undergo to understand them, and their literatures are full of problems regarding the integration and diverse readings of the texts. The mania for the "text" of a work written in a living language, particularly for a perfect "text" in Italian — a language which has not undergone appreciable variations from its birth on — is something ridiculous. It is a purely pedantic task, an end in itself, it is an effect of the German cultural invasion which is making itself felt in an untimely manner now that the Germans have already abandoned their erudite prewar mania and are giving themselves over instead to a mania for metaphysics, to arbitrary and pigheaded constructions which they erect above any commonplace argument, above any manifestation of expression and of thought whatever.

March 15, 1934

Life is like an overcoat; an overcoat which we need twenty-five years to learn how to wear. Then, after we have been comfortable inside it for twenty years, it begins to show the weave, and soon, little by little, it gets reduced to a rag.

March 16, 1934

To have been personally acquainted with Tolstoy would have been an extraordinary event, had one been able to do away completely with any thought of oneself. Probably there were days when he felt contrary — bad humor which got in the way of the pleasure of direct rapports with him; but to experience a week of life at Yasnia Polyana — to see the flow of that river of diverse, rich, rich energies, all directed toward interesting ends! Turgenev had the trappings of Parisian polish and affability, while with Dostoevsky one would have had to deal with the attacks of his infirmity; Tolstoy was the purest, the most violent and the richest.

May 21, 1934

"Rayonnement" is a word which one often uses in French to indicate a rare quality in people, a capacity for warmth, a solar capacity which irradiates from them and of which the effects are felt all around. It does not depend on the words which such people speak; it lies beyond words and thought because words and thoughts may be obvious and common but when they are moved by this force they become the condensation of an exceptional quality.

Rarer still are cases when this force is exercised postmortem. There are very few examples in history: Jesus and Saint Francis. Just what are the sayings of Jesus, the words of Saint Francis? A few signs, interpreted and related by humble people who do not communicate anything of their spoken efficacy. And yet how much they live! — even more today than for the people to whom they were spoken. Their heat has kept growing through the centuries, and with regard to the sayings of Jesus, it seems that we are barely at the start of their life.

Christian history is the history of the advent of Christ. What is the significance of the Gospels? A rudimentary testimony. Saint Paul, the only man capable of understanding

Him, never knew Him. But light pours forth continually from that naked testimony. With respect to what will happen in the future, we are still pre-Christian, as if Christ had not yet come into the world. The words which we have heard are transitory fruits, but the tree persists in its luxuriance; it will bear new fruits — the same words, made richer, more mature for the men of the future.

Primitive Christianity was entirely monopolized by Judaism, and by the strictest, most ferocious form which Judaism had taken in turning from the evils of Babylon. Thwarted in its political élan and reduced to a sort of desperate defense, it was locked in a violent reclusiveness which was both the antithesis and the product of timidity. So primitive Christianity was a doctrine of secretiveness and denial, which carried Phariseeism back to its principles in the face of the entirely exterior degeneration which had made it a paradise of arrogance and hypocrisy. The early Christians denounced hypocrites, but they enclosed themselves in the same circle of aversion and condemnation of others in which hypocrites, since the end of the heroic era, have prospered. Then the Church reacted and made peace between primitive Christianity and the world; but certainly it has no connection with primitive Christianity. Any impulses to return to her heroic ages do not carry the Church closer to Christ, they lead her farther and farther away.

May 24, 1934

In art we do not want feeling, understood as an intention superimposed on the work, like some voluntary determination on the part of the artist; it is life which is wanted, and that is that state of the soul and of the mind common to a whole time, almost an impersonal force, which the artist represents and expresses in a superior manner. Without this "vis a tergo" of the artist, this motor impulse, there is no art.

May 27, 1934

Dozens of volumes have been published which patiently conduct research on "the thought" of Shakespeare. But it is not Shakespeare's thought which is important, it is the writings.

June 1, 1934

One thing, in fact two things, were missing in the Roman Empire: the conquest of Germany and the conquest of Arabia. If the conquest, and thereby the permeation of Hellenism, had occurred in these regions too there would never have been either the barbarian invasions or the triumphs of the armies of Islam. The world of today would be the same as then, united under the standard of Rome. Standard and not dominion; differentiation among the provinces was always manifest so long as the Empire remained vital — until the time of Septimius Severus when it became transmuted into an empty organism, at the service of the Praetorian cohorts. It is not necessarily true that even under these circumstances civilization would have become tired and empty. The Egyptian civilization, which was so much less happy, lasted five thousand years; it developed its vicissitudes of decadence and of rebirth on its own, without contacts and influxes from the outside. The essentially Greek civilization, which is now ours, could have expanded through a vaster domain without losing vitality and without permitting those reverses and violent outbreaks which exhausted and at times mutilated and buried it.

Vice is something very positive which is not worth the price paid for it. The unpardonable vice is callous malevolence — the passion for paying back evil with evil. This cold-blooded determination to take vengeance at any time whatsoever is a "piatto che si mangia sempre freddo" — a dish which one always eats cold.

July 7, 1934

Sculpture is nothing but a trap for light. Thus critics make it say whatever they want; they have the works photographed the way they want and as a result photographs of sculpture never constitute an objective document, whereas of painting they do. The photographer's appraisal acts on any solid whatever, modifying its planes and its structure according to his point of reference and tricks of lighting.

The opening of the Grand Hotel in Rome signaled the change from papal Rome to Rome-les-Bains. A history should be written of that kingdom, whose king was Carlo di Rudinì and whose tutelary god was a far-off D'Annunzio.

The annoyance of Latin for me has always been the annoyance of the syntax. Where the syntax is simple, as in Caesar, I have enjoyed it right from the beginning. Ovid is very Latin, and his Latinism is badly adapted to those scenes and ceremonies of ancient folklore which he is trying to describe. Every now and then he abandons himself and there is nothing more fresh and spontaneous than those moments, but then he pulls himself together and remembers to be Latin, at which point his poetry seems like the translation of some Alexandrian poet like Callimachus.

July 8, 1934

What delights me in works from the French Renaissance is that the elaboration, the details, are Gothic. They believed they were copying Italy, but the workmen were the same as before; they had learned too well, too delicately, all those Gothic forms which were completely real to them, and they could not forget them. Thus the French monuments have something graceful and elegant about them, something alive in each minute detail, in each angle.

Andrea del Castagno is an "expressionist" of his time, who knows the human figure and is happy with it. He is also a pure calligraphist fascinated by the lineaments of faces, who derives his inspiration from the familiar and "spirited" faces of his fellow citizens, not from the deformations and intense primitivism of Negro or Oceanic Art.

Artistic creation, in relation to its creator, is like a hernia — it has the least possible zone of communication with his actual person.

One can say that one of the joys of man lies in finding himself in contact with adolescence of the spirit. Woman, the company of woman, consists of this, once the most instinctive moment of physiological pleasure has been surmounted; but in eras when women are kept in seclusion they do not mature and are not open to the life of the spirit, so the wisest and most cultivated men pursue the company of male adolescents. One class of women, perhaps — the courtesans — reached the point of satisfying this need in men and became the instrument of Hellenic civilization better and more strongly than the boys.

England for a hundred and fifty years, and the rest of the white race for a lesser period, let's say for seventy-five years, has lived in a state of full demographic inflation, imposed by the discovery of zones to populate, and by the more or less far-reaching and thorough conquest of native markets. After any inflation, deflation becomes necessary, and this is the essence of today's crisis. Belief in the value of quantity is a superstition which is quite illegitimate in terms of anything which exists today, and it only goes on in the contemporary world through inertia.

The Greeks were spurred on to their colonizing and imperialistic expeditions by the force of their vitality, and they covered — and at one time dominated — the whole of the known world, but it was an unfertile domination. As their wave retreated, the nuclei which they were able to leave in the various coastal points were too slight to hold up against pressure from the natives. The Greeks, by the very fact of their geographical origin, were very few. There could not be any more because no more could enter Greece; and they could not become more numerous because what few expatriates there were were quickly overpowered. Thus they had the function of aristocracy, and a destiny which was politically limited, but magnificent, if you consider the imprint their civilization has left.

September 22, 1934

Puritanism makes Americans feel great pride about all the things that they don't know.

All "ratés" are jealous; it is not a fault, it is a natural fact. Only a man without any ambition to succeed is free of jealousy; or else a man who has become happily successful.

Ravaisson, the French philosopher of well-merited fame, also had a mania for considering himself a great connoisseur of art. He had huge trashy canvases around in his house, and one day he was showing them to Renan. "This is a Raphael," he said, "in his early period." "Qu'il est heureux," answered Renan, "qu'il ait quitté sitôt sa première manière." [1]

September 23, 1934

Michelangelo was a ponderous, oppressive man, but not heavy. No one has attracted the attention of mediocre people more than he, and all the German art critics are mediocre.

[1] "How fortunate . . . that he abandoned his early period so soon."

Leonardo is an intellectual, and the Germans have no feeling for the facts and problems of the intellect. But the irrational, the "titanic" aspect of Michelangelo touches them to the quick; everything which in them is exaggerated, aggressive, petulant, overworked, they find expression of in him.

This morning I reached a conclusion which has great intellectual value for me, or rather cultural value. I was able to find the thread which connects the art of Easter Island — hitherto considered a mysterious and superstitious manifestation of some vanished world — with the art of Java, with Malayan art in general. And since the latter stems directly from Indian art, and Indian art is simply another manifestation of Greek art, there you have it — all the oriental world is one, which is something I had always supposed and had a presentiment of, but which only today have demonstrated to myself with exact precision.

Metternich and Bismarck do not represent the diplomatic "type"; they are great geniuses who in the history of the last century have had a vast importance — comparable to none other and impossible to reproduce. Metternich was a man who believed with all the force of his soul in the goodness of a social state which by now is destined to disappear; many people may lament that faith of his, but, given his premises, nobody can deny the wisdom of his work, though it was certainly condemned to failure. Bismarck was able to concentrate so much power in himself that the dire consequences were felt for many years after. But these are rare

men. The usual diplomats and statesmen "in power" are
people who obtain extraordinary results so long as they are
favored by circumstance; everything comes to pass, and
they do not give even the least push to events. Events today
are too complex. These people's social propaganda does not
count for anything: those pleasantly basted-together relationships, all that worldy pomp and prestige, is nothing but a
relic of the seventeenth century when politics was a dy-
nastic matter and Louis XIV sent around his agents to
spend a huge fortune giving a sensitive picture of the splen-
dors of their own monarch to foreign courts. The system of
embassies will be, I predict, abandoned very soon. They
will continue to be national political agencies, but their
aims will be in terms of more real things — economic rapport — and they will leave aside the costly pretense of maintaining their importance in society.

September 24, 1934

Very beautiful, very tall, the Marchioness of R. has had
more influence on the life of Paris and London than any
other of her contemporaries. It is she who has invented the
"Ritzonian" style (which was the boast of the Ritz before
the war) and since she had no private income, the success of
the Ritz must also have provided her with large percent-
ages. She was descended from a Suvoroff, and although she
did not know a word of Russian, a great deal of that
atavism remained in her. She had a genuine passion for
music, though anything else she felt was all approximative
and for a show: a "faux-col" culture. She was very afraid of

me; she never knew what I would throw out at her in the course of a conversation. Her company was very pleasant so long as one considered all things from a worldly, frothy point of view. Her daring consisted entirely in gallantry, not at all in things of the intellect. She was amoral as only the great English ladies know how to be, when they have become separated from their puritanical foundations. At one time she had to undergo a delicate operation and all of Paris stood by anxious and curious. While everyone was asking one another: "Mais qu'est-ce qu'elle a eu? qu'a-t-on trouvé?" Robert de Montesquiou, as soon as he knew the result, interjected: "Mais c'est bien clair: un paquet de cartes de visite." [1]

English fascination is not "charm"; one submits to fascination; it is an almost animal power with which one does not rest easy; usually one feels conquered but not persuaded. There is no true attraction in it. "Charm" on the other hand produces enduring results; it is profoundly stimulating — it helps one to live.

In the charming legend of the Pied Piper of Hamelin one finds an echo of the German migrations into Transylvania; a fact which the immediate descendants could not explain without seeing some portent in it — and in fact it must have been a migration of young adventurers who were so young as to seem children in the remembrance of them. Around the thirteenth century there happened to be great overpopula-

---

[1] "But what was the matter with her? what did they find?" . . . "But it is perfectly obvious: a packet of visiting cards."

tion throughout the Germany of that time; it was the reason for the crusading impulse, as it was for the founding of the Baltic colonies. There is the Children's Crusade among the Crusades as well. Stranger still was the fact that they went into Transylvania, a land which was so remote and apart as to give rise to the idea that there had been some magic summons, and thus the legend must have been born.

September 28, 1934

This — La Consuma[1] — is my real life. But I do like returning to Florence, because there I can do no less than be an institution, in fact the manager of an institution. And then, when I am there, I feel myself caught up to some extent in the competitive world.

November 23, 1934

Work is not profitable until one gets going with it seriously; until the surface is cracked. Broken hours, half hours snatched here and there, are all total loss. Only drunkards of work, the people who are saturated and replete from it, can succeed in working.

What a horror it would be to see the Minoan palaces as they were at the time they were built, with their crude, heavy colors and their ungraceful masses, sort of enormous barracks and mills, with such clumsy, violent and barbaric dimensions. That taste had a very brief season; too

[1] In those years Berenson used to pass the summer in a villa near La Consuma.

much history was necessary in order for it to mature. We find its having blossomed only in Egypt, after the consummation of several civilizations, and then in Athens, but there for perhaps scarcely fifty years. And then Athens; let's think for a moment of the confusion of the Acropolis — that confusion of little temples, pavilions and statues, with their fine little umbrellas of stone to protect them from bird droppings: to this was reduced the space against which the profiles of the major monuments are outlined today. A sort of muddle and chaos, a population of sculpture which was no different from the fine order and harmony that exists today in Trespiano, the modern cemetery of Florence. Space, the ideal of space, was abolished. The city sprang into being enclosed and fortified; all architected and constructed like a gratuitous stone creation in the terrible surrounding void.

Bergson will never become Catholic. He is able to approach Catholicism and accept it insofar as it is feeling and spiritual life, but never as mythology. Perhaps he could better understand mythology in the aesthetic and historical sense, as I do.

November 25, 1934
What makes me suffer in my work is not the momentary boredom and difficulty of minute research, of infinitesimal problems, of knowing to which of the numerous — and all worse than mediocre — followers of Michelangelo to attribute the drawings which I am studying; it is doubt as to the quality of my instrument. If my instrument, this tool which I

have labored so many years to temper, which in fact not I alone but each and every one of us insofar as we are dedicated to these studies have created and guarded and refined — my elders and betters and my contemporaries — if it does not serve its purpose today, then everything has been useless, and my life badly spent. It is a doubt which one cannot take lightly; only charlatans emerge from it by sneering at it. T. S. Eliot is a case in point: he continually scorns the very form of culture and intelligence on which he lives, and this is the reason why he is so unsympathetic to me, despite his many talents.

All French writers have begun by publishing a book of verse. Once it used to be said that: "Ils ont tous besoin de se plaindre de leur première maîtresse chez Lemerre." [1]

November 27, 1934

Titian and Goya, barring their respective fine points, are two journalists, and Velásquez instead is a true author. Titian demonstrates profound gifts, while Goya's qualities are much more brilliant but are qualities of pure appearance; both obtain effects which are surprising on first sight. But Velásquez is one of those summits which one learns to know better and better the closer one is to them — penetrating into ever new regions. Like Rembrandt, who of his more than a thousand canvases, is a true painter in perhaps two hundred, perhaps a dozen paintings or so could be singled

[1] "They all feel they have to bewail their first mistress at Lemerre." (Lemerre: a well-known publisher in Paris.)

out from the immense number of works by Goya. The rest is daily commentary, like the work of Sem or Daumier; and then Daumier's caricatures have yet a wholly other accent, being the expression of moral resentment.

May 26, 1935

This music by Mozart is all groomed and elaborated, quite outside of any reality. It is not that it is facile, or merely linear; it has three dimensions, but within a special space. It forms volumes, but they are crystal volumes.

May 31, 1935

When I see a modern French drawing reproduced I immediately perceive a quality so live, so piquant and elegant in the design, that I convince myself that the grand tradition of art in France has not become impoverished. One can really say that for nine centuries France has held the field with Romanesque and Gothic architecture and sculpture, with the sculpture of the late Renaissance, with all the arts from the Grand Siècle on, blossoming so diversely as the Rococo in the eighteenth century and in the nineteenth century as the great and very serious modern painting. From Ingres and David to Degas, or rather to Cézanne and Matisse, it is an age of gold — a richness and a strength which has been unequaled. Italy did take first place from her twice: first with Giotto, and then for a hundred years, let us even say for a hundred and fifty years, with that painting which we can call "fifteenth century."

Did Venice supersede France in the eighteenth century? No. Venice was essentially French. She possessed a painter of great talent, Tiepolo; an enchanting decorator, so full of air, of light, of flight; but not essentially a painter. He had no primal force. As for Guardi, it is not true that he is a miracle of modernity; he is not a precocious impressionist. Guardi painted the way other people touched-up and sketched. His novelty lay in his not finishing the picture; he gives us, in what he paints, the freshness and immediacy which first existed in the sketched drawing.

My work, the little work which I do every day, I could consider, at the very most, worth ten lire. Since I spend a thousand in any day, I am exploiting nine hundred and ninety lire. I am not ashamed of it; I am making a factual observation. This possibility of exploitation — the unjust freedom to make use of wealth — unjust from the point of view of the "homo oeconomicus" — conditions culture, and civilization — conditions all those forms of life which are dear to me and which I believe in, and which I believe to be useful, in the final analysis, to the whole of humankind, even to those whom some people consider and commiserate with as "having been exploited."

June 1, 1935
Velásquez accepts his characters as they present themselves to him, and then he reconstructs them from within — he creates them, he does not copy them or photograph them, which would be impossible for an artist, but at the same time

he does not impose himself on them. He has no preconceptions. El Greco has a fixed decorative scheme in his eye and works out exercises continually along a single scale. Rembrandt is free with respect to his methods of expression, but his sphere of feeling is occupied; he has an internal need for grandeur, for the heroic, for the epic, which he betrays in his art. Titian and Tintoretto also possess this heroic scheme, and besides that possess an aristocratic sense which was not part of Rembrandt. Velásquez is perhaps the first artist to have made himself human when faced with the human form, and many painters who derive from him learned this intention without fully and genuinely possessing it as he did: Manet, for example. But in all the followers there is something more restricted than there is in him: artistic liberty for them becomes simply a way to interpret.

Velásquez is a purely Italian painter, but one who inherited and learned the Italian artistic methods at a time in which Italians had already lost their intrinsic warmth and force and were reduced to the scope of decoration and scenic design: church painting and salon painting. He ushers in an extraordinary vigor and freshness, so that he is really an Italian painter but one whom Italy was no longer capable of producing — after Caravaggio and Ribera! It is exactly comparable to the case which Wilamovitz cites of the Alexandrian poets, who had become reduced to an empty elegance but were reborn in Italy through the fresh energy of Catullus, Propertius and Tibullus. It is also the case of Spenser, who translated the already tired and relatively adulterated Ronsard and Du Bellay into English poetry which, although born of the French, is better and more vivid than the original. Distance and geographical novelty are the cause of this portentous renovation. How could one define the painting of Velásquez? Naturalistic? Visualistic? It simply has the quality of great painting — painting which has digested technique, painting in which the vehicle of expression disappears. To say it is naturalistic makes it seem that you mean it is what the common man would want, whereas no man who was not Velásquez could have imagined it as it is. It is a created thing, but created according to a model, a fully human idea, and thus never preconceived but intrinsic with the aspects of the reality which it depicts.

June 3, 1935

Celsus and Proclus instigated absolutely rational attacks on Christianity. They expressed reason's repulsion of the Christian myths vehemently and pertinaciously, but without any blindness or hatred. But what did it amount to? The whole of humanity was passing through a phase of irrationalism, everyone was moving along on a "tapis roulant" which was carrying them as far from reason as possible, so the opposite road taken by those two sages amounted to nothing; their efforts were entirely in vain. Voltaire added nothing new to their arguments, he showed no greater persuasive force, but he marched with the general current, and each of his steps marked progress on everybody's part. His own movement was strengthened by the universal motion. There was no major value intrinsic in him, except that of perfect timeliness.

Full and perfect art is that which seeks out and studies human forms; the nude pure and simple, or awareness of the nude under draperies, the feeling of the nude which enlivens clothed bodies. When clothing only carries an emphasis on pleats and drapery the field of art is limited and what develops is the sense of landscape, as in Chinese art. But Gothic art brought its bodies to life inside their clothing, and Romanesque art, with its caricature and grotesque figures, represented an exasperation with the corporeal — a sort of ardent, lovesick search for tactile values through deformation, above and beyond all anatomical precision.

June 4, 1935

Originality is a manifestation of incompetence.

June 7, 1935

Goya is a rapid, nervous draftsman, but he is not a great draftsman. He is an artist riddled with Mannerism, but it is something different from the usual mannerism of his time, from that of Parmigianino's followers. So he passes for a great innovator, as though he were the first of the realists. He is not a realist but a brutalist; he has no more contact with reality than his emulators, except to the extent that he violates it.

July 28, 1935

The universe is full of currents, all unknown and mysterious; it is like the center of an enormous confusion. Its scientific explanations, which were so much in style at the time of my youth, are only myths; they have no greater reality (except perhaps a slightly larger field of observation) than Thomistic philosophy. We human beings in the universe are more or less the momentary condensers of these shapeless, inscrutable, and innumerable currents; we are aware of them as foreshadowings, or as obscure remembrances, but we do not know how to follow them, and when we do hold to them they carry us toward chaos. Science seeks to enlarge the circle of human light, but it does not "explain" anything; it does not declare, it does not arrive at any fixed point and limit. It, too, continually fashions myths, and they have the profound value of convictions, until the moment when they are substituted by others which are more convincing. Myth began with the savages, as terror and taboo, then it became "theoform," then anthropomorphic, then mechanistic, then mathematic, and now it is returning little by little to bathe in the uncertain and the mysterious. The history of science is, if understood in its strictest sense, the history of this myth.

July 31, 1935

Cretan art is like the spontaneous blossoming of an art which is not yet set, crystallized and made geometric — this being a stage through which it would have to pass before becoming truly mature. Thus it possesses a natural elegance, but also a natural foolishness, grace, and almost accidental élan, to the detriment of more solid qualities, so that the recent decadent attempts to revive it are as silly as they can possibly be, like baby talk in a grown woman. The Cretan artists preferred (and one might also say that they knew nothing else) an undulating, sinuous line — a line to which the eye is carried because it is instinctively easy and pleasing, partaking of a fresh, newborn sensuality. We see this in the agile and surprising movements of their beasts, and also in these deformations of the human figure corseted in so very tightly so that there is a necessity for undulation, for movement, for making that otherwise almost perpendicular line of the body vibrate.

August 8, 1935

To return to my daily poison: the more I study Michelangelo the more I see that it was a single constant force which moved him at seventeen and impelled him for sixty years, right into his extreme old age. The content of his work may change but the motivation is always that one — identical — always carrying the same intensity — always present. Why does he happen to possess it? And who can answer this question? His family was rather craven; of some nobility, but of the lowest, qualifiable for very modest dispensations from the state. His city, if one can extract a character from it, had the character of subtle and tired intelligence, already turned back on itself in the form of universal skepticism. One of his contemporaries, Guicciardini, is full of acute awareness of things, a just sense of proportion and a spirit adequate for any criticism, while Michelangelo on the other hand is unchained force, turgid immensity of form, excessive desire. What he had in him he expressed from the very first things he did, and his decrepitude was never enough to make him exhaust it, or to give him the desire or the possibility of changing. Nobody can be asked to change against his own nature; it cannot be asked today of Moravia, no matter how angry one may get with his talent. One cannot presume to substitute one's own taste for the exigencies of a living person.

For centuries the Jews have continued to await the Messiah and for this reason they have never become a nation.

August 9, 1935
Whoever creates a philosophical system abandons skepticism. I myself, taken with the taste and the need of a relative skepticism, have never been able to imprison myself in any system. Whenever I have begun to create one I have immediately destroyed it; it can only be of value to me as a mental fiction. But there is too much uncertainty, too much movement in me and in things, for me to find an explanation of them in some fixed and peremptory form, which is what a system is.

People maintain that spontaneity and artistic worth all depend on breaking conventions. They don't know that once they are broken, new ones have to be fabricated. It would be as though each time I had to draw water I set out to make a new pitcher.

August 13, 1935
Like Moravia, Flaubert was prey to an obsession that his world was bleak and sordid, and when he tried to move out of it he was unable to do anything but evade it in a ponderous

and mechanical phantasmagoria; he passed from the mysteries of the darkroom to the cooking of mock turtle soup.

August 15, 1935
Moravia's last novel, *Le Ambizioni Sbagliate* is a beautiful wild beast, dangerous to itself and to others.

The ferocity of the Renaissance was a personal factor which went along with the civilization of that epoch, with the tone of that culture; today ferocity is abstract and organized. Thus there has been moral progress, for now ferocity does not enter at all into the character of an individual; whoever exercises it does so in the spirit of a functionary, not a man of parties and vendettas.

August 18, 1935
Flaubert was a lyricist who lacked the force to compose poems.

The painters of today are people with whom it is impossible to have relationships, unless you are one of them; outside of their own craft they accept nobody but a critic who praises them or a patron who pays them. They have all segregated themselves off into the egoism of their own genius, into the cult of their romanticism. At one time this was not true; in the Renaissance they were not artists but artisans, and a city like Florence had an entire population of artisans. The feudal lords had been conquered; the Medici, until the time of the Grand Duchy, were considered equal to everyone else, if not in power, in quality, and thus "character," in relationships, triumphed above all. Leo X or Clement VII trembled before the "genius" of Michelangelo — not the genius of the artist, but the power, the vehemence of the man.

The vogue for the Baroque in our time was created by the Germans with their mania for what there is in it of the complicated, the extraordinary, the trumped-up, the original. Aspects which in the art of that time, the end of the fifteenth century and the sixteenth century, nobody had ever dreamed of affirming with perfect cognizance. Art of the late Renaissance, one can call it, or more simply of the sixteenth century. It was outstanding in its good artists, deteriorated in the mediocre ones, and was sometimes offensive, as in the Spanish, or in Naples and Sicily, but never in Rome. One can say that the danger lay in its being too much "sauce" — too much sauce and too little roast — or in its rhetorical amplification of the Renaissance scheme, which was so simple and thus so quickly became insipid.

The future is only an adjective; the present has substantive value. What we call the future is a modification of the present state of our soul — either of desire or of fear.

August 20, 1935
English painters of the nineteenth century lack any spontaneous impulse and artistic ingenuousness. They are people with too much culture and too many thoughts, theories and abstractions, and despite their technical proficiency, the

value of their painting is always merely illustrative — illustrative of their theories or their banally pleasant emotions, or, as is the vogue today, illustrative of disgusting emotions which the upbringing of the past used to hide. The English are curious; absolutely incapable of theorizing about things which are important to them, and full of theories about things which, substantially, are devoid of any reality for them.

The best quality in mystical spirits lies in their establishing spontaneous and immediate contact with people and things; but there is also the impulse in them to push themselves beyond this individual experience and to believe in a metaphysical and objective reality or in a form of magic which governs everything. In general things go badly between me and them, because they find me happy and in full accord with the immediate contact, but invincibly opposed to believing in the objective magical reality. For me it is a world from which I have emerged, like the warm maternal lap, and I cannot succeed in imagining a process of involution whereby I would be able to readapt to it.

Dialectic is an excellent (more than perfect, more than regular) instrument, similar to those hydraulic wheels which draw the water out of a ditch and then pour it back, from all the equally full buckets, into the same ditch once the cycle has been completed. It leaves, therefore, everything in its place and does not serve any purpose at all except to demonstrate its own precise excellence.

October 4, 1935

When I came to Italy, the center of my interests — that which caught me immediately and spoke to me — was Venetian painting. I approached the rest of Italian art through an initial effort of attention and through an intellectual process, but it was enough for me to see the great Venetian masters once to be exalted and transported by them. It has been said that Titian's *Education of Love* recalls certain groups of figures from the Pompeian Villa of the Mysteries, but there is an even more profound resemblance. As Greek art is a summit of human creative achievement, so also is Venetian painting; it is an act of aesthetic purity which no longer has any intellectual mediation. Florentine art has extraordinary force and elegance, but in those early days it did not persuade me; I felt it was too Gothic.

If only Andrea del Sarto had been born in Venice! But the material fact of birth means nothing; if he had been educated by the great Venetian masters, by someone like Bellini, he would have been a painter very close to Titian, and just as great. Unfortunately his talent had to be exercised on excellent academic models from which any direct vital inspiration had already vanished, to be replaced by a rhetorical, intellectual formula, and his genius was not enough to break it and renovate it.

October 6, 1935

English poetry is the only form of art which comes close to Italian painting. Seeing canvases by Tintoretto I find verses from Keats coming to mind. And it is not the resemblance of subject matter — autumnal nature, golden sunsets, heavenly flights and triumphs — which at times one encounters between painter and poet; it is the same emotion and aesthetic excellence, the same voice of the spirit.

Here is a Florentine who was not a good enough sculptor to be employed in Florence, who came up here and did as enchanting a thing as this group in the corner of the Ducal Palace.[1] Here he used a Phidian perfection of line to carry out a Gothic idea — that of marrying architectonic forms to sculpture, of grouping the figures in such a way as to avail himself of the corner — and out of it came something extremely graceful: figures in calm, collected attitudes full of humanity and of tranquil sensuality. Here are two qualities with which Florence was quite unacquainted, and how precious they must be to our soul. By dint of dryness, of sinew, Florentine art quickly achieved its peak — the lean, purely intellectual elegance of Donatello, for example. It was not enriched by other elements, and thus it lasted very little time. Already by 1530 it was finished; the Michelangelo of the period following the Medici Tombs makes frightening and overpowering works — no longer beautiful things.

October 15, 1935
To give motion to a painting it is no use to conduct an accurate study of the human figure, or at least it is not enough;

[1] He is referring to the corner capital with the *Judgment of Solomon* near the Porta della Carta of the Ducal Palace in Venice; a work signed "Duo sotii florentini" (Two Florentine associates).

you need muscular imagination. The study and knowledge of anatomy can have negative value; it can correct some imaginative error, but if imagination does not give the cue for the painting, then nothing moves — there are only chilly contortions.

October 16, 1935

Pure pictorial value is that which is found in Paolo Veronese — much more than that of Tintoretto, more even than Titian, who transcends mere painting to manifest something heroic, tempestuous. Veronese gives me joy; I can contemplate him at length with an equal and constant impression, like a great spectacle with no drama, magnificent but so natural that it is not scenographic. It is a beautiful spread of painting, dense and compact, it is not superficial — it is animal, rather — giving to the figures that perfect weight and equilibrated structure which is a physical gift. Animality frankly felt is not a superficial fact; on the other hand what is superficial is a falsely spiritual intention which empties and torments forms without transfiguring them.

Literary and humanistic studies, not technical practice, are what prepare one for a taste and understanding for pictures. Whoever has read many of the classics is far advanced in a world of figurations and myths which of necessity transform themselves into images — the same images which have brought artistic creations to life. By so doing one is already attuned to the world of art right from its archaic roots and its blossoming among the Greeks. On the other hand a man who has only the practice of painting is all taken up with technical, practical and momentary problems and does not know how to see; and not only does he not know how to see the work of art, he does not see the natural spectacle either; he can see only his own colors and his own canvas.

November 12, 1935

Architecture has a very limited language, with obligatory elements which close it off; for instance the necessity and the proximity of the angles. It is more scenographic than the other arts; that is, it develops in the mind of whoever looks at it, more than it strikes his sensibility. Of architectural interiors, perhaps only the Greek cross resolves everything into an immediate impression; with the Latin (Roman) cross one enters into the field of theater and perspective.

November 20, 1935

Sebastiano del Piombo is nothing but a wide-awake youth who apprenticed himself to Giorgione in the same way that he might have become apprenticed to a stone mason or a blacksmith, and he learned the trade showing an incontestable capability. Between his youthful and rhetorical (insofar as it was not based on a live feeling for form or on any destiny of genius) capability and Michelangelo's heroic impulse there was not such a great distance. However, Michelangelo was almost lying in wait for gifted young artists and it is understandable that from the moment he saw one spring up nearby he saw in him his predestined pupil, the continuator of his work. But that capability of Sebastiano's led to nothing more than a love for elegant and ornamental beauty of clothes and accessories.

November 21, 1935

Ruskin believed he was only interested in art insofar as it was illustration, for its evocative capacity and its literary representation, but he was too much of a genius to stop at this point in his investigations, and he was more than aware of whatever, in any work of art, was really art, at least up to the point that his brutish prejudices based on the Bible allowed him to be. Thus Michelangelo to him was simply first and foremost a pagan; his excessive love of form, the nude understood as essential form, clashed, so it seems, with Ruskin's Christian sentiments; certainly it clashed with his Presbyterian upbringing. Tintoretto, however, is a magnificent Biblical subjectist. Furthermore he realized his visions principally through color (and color is the visual element through which Ruskin felt most exalted) and his nudes are bathed, absorbed in light to such an extent that as a result they are obliterated.

November 22, 1935

It is perfectly justifiable to take crucifixes as a subject for art criticism, as Mrs. Vavalà has done. Christ on the cross is like a form of language: obligatory and slowly evolving. The difference from a literary language lies really in this: that the limits of artistic language are much more restricted, the elements being fewer — thus individual variation is less admissible, so that one only becomes aware of it to any notable degree at some distance of time. Speaking to the masses in images is a much less articulate sort of work than writing; decades and centuries are necessary before the masses adapt themselves to any appreciable change due to this sort of discourse. Sacred art survived so long as this contact with the population remained possible, and the last great painter to speak from the altars is Rubens; Rubens after the Council of Trent, when, therefore, he was personifying the last word, the final position of the Church. From that time on, the Church has not budged, and because of this immobility it has lost its life. No longer finding the way to a manifestation in art means simply this: losing contact and losing life.

April 2, 1936

American pedantry is skyscraper pedantry; German pedantry only reaches the seventh or eighth floor. American philologers and "scientists" are like the storyteller who, when the bandit king offered his daughter and half his kingdom to anyone who would recount him an unending story so as to entertain his leisure for the rest of his life, presented himself to the sovereign and began to narrate: "Once upon a time there was a beehive, and into it there went a bee, and then another bee, and another bee, and another bee, and another bee" and he went on like this for days. "But," said the king, "when are you going to begin telling me the story?" "When the bees have finished going in." "And when will the bees have finished going in?" "Never."

Performance should blunt, shade, mute whatever is violent and emotional in dramatic texts, because when the written word of the drama stands before us in the nudity of the print and strikes us directly with its open force it is a blow which we can stand, but drama on the stage reaches us with the support of colors, gestures, the sound of the voice, mimicry — all prohibited blows. To balance the effect the actor's concern must be entirely for reduction and mitigation.

April 3, 1936
A perfect critical knowledge of art is necessary in order to falsify works of art successfully. The falsifiers are in effect critics who have not resigned themselves to their expository profession, but have gone on as far as feigned creation. And sometimes between this and genuine creation the step is so short that to escape the deception one needs an absolutely extraordinary acuteness or persistence of gaze.

April 7, 1936
When I created the "Amico di Sandro" I was not bold enough. I tried to give this artistic personality some basis in a real person, albeit a person who was unknown according to the documents. But artistic personality is something in itself, which is detached from the real person and lives autonomously, so the group of works which I have attributed to the "Amico di Sandro" do not partake of the work of Botticelli and Filippino Lippi, but "traverse" them, the way "quanta" meteorically traverse matter.

May 10, 1936

Because aristocrats and the common man are genuine races they are exempt from vulgarity. Vulgarity is a privilege of the middle class. But the many aristocrats who are vulgar beat any other vulgarity, because they flavor it with a special arrogance which makes it more aggressive and more showy.

May 11, 1936

When scientists and learned men do not have a universal and creative mind but are "specialists," they are people whose lives and interests have been reduced to such a thin thread that the one exercise they can do is to dance along a tightrope.

May 12, 1936

Criticism is like the drop which keeps falling insistently and wears away the hardest stone. There is no idea ever expressed which does not have a future; it is just that the life of a man is too short a span, so that within it much which eventually will have development and consequences seems to be useless, wasted, and lost.

In conducting their investigations the Greeks considered everything as being independent from everything else, since the time of Thales, and on this presupposition they laid the groundwork for the whole structure of human reason; for twenty-five centuries people have kept laboring, and one can feel satisfied with the results. But the Chinese, like any

other primitive people, have always maintained their faith
in the harmony of the universe; they have never separated
either the objects which they were observing, or man, from
nature; they have always held the position that we call mystical, and have constructed their science on this basis, which
we do not consider scientific. Thus, in choosing a place to
build a house, they investigate the water and the winds and
thereby believe they are arriving at as practical a result as
we do when we cling to our calculations of stability.

May 18, 1936

Criticism can do nothing but point out the beautiful wherever it finds it, unless it enters into particular disquisitions
on the "parts" of a work, as Matthew Arnold does in *On
Reading Homer,* or Sainte-Beuve does for French poetry
of the sixteenth century. Any other discourse on beauty is
metaphysical, or, in the more banal cases, gossips which even
if they do not succeed in being damning to anyone who has
any sense, at least succeed in being useless. However, they
do have one valuable point, which is that of holding one's attention. When they enter the spirit they induce it into a
state which I would call posthypnotic, without which the
eyes would not see and the ears would not hear, or would
not have the illusion of seeing or of hearing. What does the
Englishman of middle class culture do who is not moved
either by aesthetic snobbery or by a pure mania for tour-
ism? He comes to the Uffizi and reads his Ruskin; he reads
the book and does not look at the picture — his mind is
all on the printed word — but he is still under the illusion

of seeing it and, in some way, he has seen it: through the suggestivity of the word he has participated in a "visual" sentiment or in the results and deductions produced by that sentiment, all of which he would never have succeeded in fomenting by himself.

The "material" in all this[1] which is the landscape and, one could say, the Nature of the Renaissance, is the most subtle possible, is reduced to the bare minimum, is a pure vehicle of expression. Material predominates when times become barbaric and art decadent. One then has the colossal, the sumptuous, the complicated, or even the polished and smooth, in an utter paroxysm of displayed material: from the barbarian sculptures to the mosaics whose gold backgrounds set off the preciosity of their polychrome marbles, right down to our own bleak, rational architecture.

May 26, 1936

Maeterlinck is a cultivator of the tragic sense "à propos de bottes."

When I undertake a new work, not a reworking or some research problem, but a work which signifies the result of much thought and of a long elaboration on my part, I feel as though I were undergoing the torments of Saint Erasmus, whose intestines were slowly drawn out by being rolled like a cable around a wheel.

[1] The surroundings of Settignano.

May 30, 1936

In every number of the *Gazette des Beaux Arts* I receive there is a beautiful reproduction of a modern drawing inside, and I am held, fascinated, amazed every time by the power of those lines. They are inevitably Parisian drawing, not French, for there is no tradition of modern art which the whole of France can boast. Only in Paris does artistic excellence persist, and it reveals itself almost uniquely in the drawings: it is like an accumulated reserve of possibilities which is not poured out into a great work, at least I don't know of one. But art is not dead so long as it lives on in this way; in fact one may say that it is in full bloom. Involution would have to show itself in the very details which today still, on the contrary, continue to be so alive, elegant, vibrant. Elsewhere, in Italy for example, modern drawing is finished off by a line which has the quality of cut leather, but this other line is all spirit and fire. When it comes to paintings, these same artists show up poorly because in this day and age the external contribution — the atmosphere, or social stability — is lacking. Composition is either nonexistent or academic, and really it had already been impeded by the chaotic, or ill-defined social conditions of the great French nineteenth century. An occasional example of valid composition is given by exotic, almost dreamlike transposition: Gauguin. But absence of compositional qualities is not synonymous with absence of imagination. If by imagination you mean fantasy, there was very little in the late nineteenth century, but if one means on the other hand greater penetration into things, greater, even supernatural, possession of the pictorial material, the nineteenth century is the century which is characterized by precisely this form of creative imagination: from Degas to Cézanne. It is this way of imagining which continues to pervade the quality of drawing; it is the ascetic, lean nobility of the artists of our own time.

December 8, 1936

It is an idle matter to bewail the lack of "beauty" in the style of modern writers; beauty is no longer an attribute either of writers or of modern civilization (which instead leans, wholesale, in the direction of expressing the Truth) and whoever looks for it today makes it into a superstructure, an archaism — or else falls into a sort of exaggeration of the gross and monstrous which replaces the tragic and the sublime, like Céline. There are certain echoes and tones of "beauty" which are no longer supportable in present-day works. It is easy for the men of today to say what they know and what they think, but very difficult for them to express what they feel. Not because they do not feel (all human beings know moments of acute and overwhelming feeling) but because something stands in the way of their expression of feeling.

One of the last writers to express himself "beautifully" was Conrad, because he wrote about adventures on the sea and the sea is still a subject which can inspire tones of song, especially in England; but nobody in this day and age could "sing" about the earth. Henry James constructed, instead, a style of absolutely artificial arabesques for himself — a style which adheres to nothing and represents nothing except the effort and the elegance with which he develops it. This lack of any beautiful style represents the breaking of a tradition; nor are there symptoms in it of a rebirth, since probably what will be reborn will be something altogether different from anything we have known and enjoyed.

Moravia's second novel, *Le Ambizioni Sbagliate*, is a baroque work — baroque in the way *Le Rouge et le Noir* is, for example. The characters are exaggerated, forced, held to one note; the figures are in too strong relief and seem contorted. This is also true of Michelangelo's *Captives*. Contortion — I would almost say the nonequanimity of lines — is a characteristic of the Baroque, and Michelangelo is baroque, beginning with his tondo in the Uffizi. What matters most to him about the figure of the Madonna? That everything converge in a spiral, and so the Child lies in her arms like a sort of pinwheel which accentuates the sense of the spiral even more. And what has this spiral figure to do with a representation of the Holy Family? This sort of thing does not occur in the peaceful plastic works which have clear meaning and feeling; they are accepted as they are without any convention beyond that of the material: i.e., that the marble of Phidias' statues be considered flesh. Bernini is not baroque: his figures are agitated, not contorted, and his great architectonic projects (the Colonnade of Saint Peter's and the Colonnade of the Louvre) are purely classical. Tuscany is a non-baroque island precisely because it is the center of the humanistic classicism of the Renaissance. Violent peoples are naturally also "baroque": Germany and Spain.

In literature the Baroque, without identifying itself with romanticism, heralds and often accompanies it. Heinze with his *Ardinghello* is a prototype of this; then there followed Schiller. In France a magnificent and almost complete example is Barbey d'Aurevilly.

December 11, 1936

In my youth, when old Frizzoni was still going around visiting museums and I had the opportunity of accompanying him, I used to be perhaps even more full of sudden enthusiasms than I am now. One day at Villa Borghese, before the Ortolano *Pietà*, I allowed myself to be swept by a transport of admiration and abandoned myself to expressions of rapture. Frizzoni, who had a perfect eye for artistic things but very little brain (as opposed to the many people today who have large brains and thereby believe they can conduct art criticism without any eye at all) interrupted me immediately: "Now let's look at these stones for a moment." They were certain stones at the base of the painting which were, according to Frizzoni, the clear sign of the hand of the artist.

If by Orient we mean our Orient — that is, the Aegean and the land around it which comprises all of Asia Minor as far as Mesopotamia — it is true that Roman art is oriental art. It is true but it is superfluous to say so, because there is no Roman art in itself, but rather a manifestation in Rome of that art which was ecumenical (as is the art of today — as any art which truly matters always is) and which was born more to the east of Rome, in the Aegean, was alive in Greece, was

alive in Asia and when, for a century and a half Rome had
centralized her political power, was alive in Rome — only to
then rediscover its center once again a little more to the east.
But beyond Mesopotamia, no; if you want to maintain that
the cradle of art, or of certain forms of art, was Armenia, or
perhaps Persia, or Turkestan, I rebel. This civilization of ours
is Greek, it is Aegean-Mediterranean, and it makes no difference that certain infinitesimal variations are met with first
in one place rather than in another; it would only be of archeological, not aesthetic interest to insistently define them
and conduct research as to their origins. Rome is oriental in
this sense: it is a province of the East, just as America today
is spiritually part of Europe, and is provincial in the same
way. In all the aesthetic fields except perhaps literature
(though even there, if you pay close attention), Roman
novelty was more a novelty of terrain than anything else; the
fresh terrain of a new language substituted for one which was
already so used and worn out that it had reached the point
of being frail and almost rumpled. Callimachus, Apollodorus,
were plants — miserable seedlings — which took root again
and found unhoped-for vigor when transported onto the new
soil. Roman poetry consists of this happy transplanting of
Callimachus.

In Leonardo one does not find that space which I love in
Perugino's and Raphael's paintings — space which helps
the body to breathe and thereby helps the spirit to live. Leonardo creates a suggestive landscape, a dream land like the
background of the *Gioconda,* but "spatial" space is a real

thing to those other painters — a live entity in the same way that bodies are; so it is not used just to create the effect of distance or removal, as, for example another Leonardesque "space" does — the one behind the head of Christ in *The Last Supper*. I would define Raphael's space as a sheath for the soul. In any case these are things which one feels but which are undefinable, and one can only communicate them by analogy.

January 6, 1937

The "visual power" of a painter has nothing to do with his painting, and here I mean visual power in the physiological sense, the oculistic defects of his vision, or in any case whatever relationship there is is of no interest. Whatever forms a painter? His artistic education in the first place, that training which (if it is a case of true and formidable talent) he has undergone enthusiastically since childhood, or to which he has submitted as a necessary yoke or compulsory chain in order to reach the goal he has set himself: to be a painter. Then there is his personal reaction to his education, and it is this which is a sign of the force of his talent, of the strictly personal element of his art. There are no physical conditions which could influence his falling away from whatever force of talent he might have. Physical conditions are a pure accident, and results can be very varied in different individuals for whom the physical conditions are identical, because of their serving the "thing in itself" which is talent; so defects of vision in a painter may interest the oculist, but not the critic, or the admirers of his painting.

There was a great fuss at one point about El Greco's astigmatism, but El Greco, the strangeness of El Greco, is one of the most explainable and patent things in the history of painting. El Greco was formed by the traditions of Byzantine icon painting, a late and clearly mannerist tradition. He then passed to Venice, under the tutelage of Tintoretto, whose example he doggedly forced himself to emulate, but he was unable to succeed entirely, or at least did not succeed in solidly uniting the two teachings in any harmonious way. Once he arrived in Spain he had free territory and an emotional climate which was favorable to his passion for painting. No one told him anything anymore, no one showed him anything anymore; he remained under his own jurisdiction, ruled by his own preferences, by his own identification with those disparate and "learned" elements of his own art which lived on to excess, in a sort of paroxysm, farther and farther removed from reality. El Greco's hallucination is a mental fact, that is to say a clear and necessary product of "his" own tradition, which was quite separate from the tradition of his contemporaries, and thus from the common standard, and thus from the tone of his epoch — all of which makes him seem exceedingly singular, particularly to anyone who confuses him with a band of painters to whom he does not belong.

January 8, 1937

The books I have read have almost all gone from my memory; they are confused with my being, leaving no trace, like the cretaceous creatures in the dunes around Folkestone.

The white cliffs are clearly visible, but who can find the single shells, reduced by now to a very fine dust, which have formed them? In the same way the books I have read have formed my mind and my culture, but their individual unity has been dispersed and no effort of memory would ever be able to put them together again for me.

January 23, 1937

It is too bad that D'Annunzio does not know how to write; he only knows how to sing. Sometimes the song is recitative, but it is never that plain discourse which does not stop with the beauty of one page but keeps itself alive throughout the whole duration of a book.

January 29, 1937

I owe eternal gratitude to William James who, through his writings, made me understand before I had reached my twenties that in order to liberate oneself from metaphysic one had to be immersed in it and study it thoroughly.

April 5, 1937

Amy Lowell was an American poetess, but poetry counted for nothing in her ambition, which was entirely taken up with aristocratic arrogance, and arrogance of a typically American stamp — extraordinarily disdainful, because genealogy in America goes no farther back than the second generation.

The world is composed only of one's own contemporaries; I mean to say that in every moment of life only one's peer group counts, and one makes no reckoning of the others, so that the external world changes color and tone according to our changes of age; it is always the same age as we are. Always, except when the threshold of old age has been crossed, because then, if you are really old, and nothing else but old, the world loses its color, becoming wan and pale. If, on the other hand, one continues to be alive, it means that we ourselves revive in ourselves experiences from the other ages which we have known in our life. This is the only way to be rejuvenated, and it is conceded to very few.

At one point in his poetry Carducci was a cold Parnassian; the poet of his "Hellenic springtimes," of that forced classicism which opened the way for his new so-called "barbaric" forms. At that time his warm, moving and compassionate inspiration (as seen in the letters to Lydia which have now been published) congealed, and the poetry which resulted was far removed from his feeling; it was a mirrored light. This would never happen to a pure classicist whose experience of feeling is already Olympian, and who has no need to pass it through a refrigerator.

In the words which William James spoke one day when he was already an old man one can recognize a symptom and a symbol of his illogicality and his polemic against precise thinking: "I am always on the lookout for an interruption."

April 8, 1937
This is a strange fact: that one cannot obtain, or can almost never obtain, any historical inquiry for the greatest of

all historical revolutions, the one which is still pervading modern times and which, for the next five thousand years, let us say, will continue to be in existence. There are infinite numbers of fanatic-exhortative-theological tales about it, from two opposite directions: the Christian apologia and the most recent pseudo-rationalist apologia. It means that nobody knows, historically, the spiritual foundations of our history. After all this time that has been dominated by the Christian revolution, nobody knows the precession of the equinoxes.

April 9, 1937

What Degas lacks is the courage to complete a work. So all his work is reduced to a series of preparatory sketches, as though Michelangelo, or even a lesser artist like Pontormo, had left nothing but drawings. This reluctance of painters to confront nobility of composition is the evil of all modern painting. Where there is no composition really there is no peak of artistry. Men like Degas, who feel that they cannot achieve it, are at least more frank and genuine, and do not make vain, rhetorical attempts, or try to camouflage.

All his works are sketches, studies for a great work, but they actually are not studies for anything. They contain the greatest mastery, there is a fullness to them, and complete efficacy of detail; they render as no other painting does the vital freedom of certain muscular movements. So one is left with the regret that this power was not enclosed and resolved within a work which always seems to be being promised. He remained too obstinately rebellious against the classical formula, which had become translated into academicism, but whose full strength he should have rediscovered.

The question of "exhibitionism" in art should be understood in a way which is detached from the personality of the creator and from the degree to which his intentions are dubious. Artists (painters) who are exhibitionists — who want to scandalize and "épater le bourgeois" — are very much fewer than there seem to be; and whatever the intimate incentive of the artist may be, his position of "sincerity" or of "falseness" before his own work does not matter at all. The sincerity of which one speaks when referring to a work of art means its internal coherence, the power of conviction which it contains. There are traces of "insincerity" — elements which are too flattering, elements of compromise — in the paintings of Sargent, but nobody could ever accuse him of having been, at heart, an exhibitionist. Boldini exploited certain particulars of his artistic vision to an extreme degree, both economically and in his pursuit of fame, but this vision was genuine in its origins. Lenbach represented the ideal between sentimental pomposity and banal aestheticism of those good mothers of the pure German race (who are willingly seen bejeweled and imposing, and yet touched at the same time with languor, like upper-class romantic prostitutes) but one cannot call him exhibitionistic or insincere, because probably his success lay precisely in the degree to which he became one with it all and believed in it without reservation. In another field, when Wagner first appeared in America he was greeted by the loudest outcries on the part of confirmed musicomanes, as though he were a mere histrionic, and certainly nobody today would say that Wagner's artistic impulse was exhibitionistic, or that his incentive was simply a desire to amaze. Perhaps the new artists seem the most exhibitionistic to us, but also and conversely, many people who are hailed as new artists are nothing but incoherent exhibitionists.

The puritan is someone who throws ashes on any aesthetic sensation whatever, in order to succeed in completely losing his taste for it.

Ability is like a ruptured hernia, which has nothing to do with either the intelligence or the character of individuals; it is often the privilege of idiots.

April 10, 1937

Any materialistic attitude is worldly, to my way of thinking. And when I say materialistic, the fact does not escape me that "worldliness" includes a strong element of elegance, but it is an elegance which one also finds within the scope of animals; think to what refinements of elegance horses can be trained. According to me, everything which one does for an advantage is materialistic and almost bestial, even when it be for a so-called moral advantage such as the value of prestige. Whoever tend toward bestiality I consider worldly, no matter in what condition they find themselves or what their aspirations may be in the social scale: the followers of the "flesh and the devil." [1]

There is however a worldliness which is an end unto itself, disinterested, and consisting of pure elegance; this ceases to be "worldly" to me and attains an aesthetic value. It may be anti-economical, superficial, and perhaps even anti-hygienic; it may keep a person from displaying any other activities (and activities which might be better in themselves); but so long as it maintains its disinterestedness and is not a means for arriving at ulterior ends, it embraces the virtues of contemplation and saves any being who practices it from utilitarianism. If worldliness is accepted as a pattern of life and as a spectacle, welcome to it; in such a case it is even immune from vanity. But the truly worldly person is looking for some advantage in any of his activities, or for unjust glorification of his own success which involves the abasement of others and delight in their humiliation.

The Catholic Church, which is the best regulator of these matters, gives excellent dispensation for worldliness. It elevates the animal acts — birth, death, copulation — to the level of sacraments, creating around them the greatest possible spiritual halo; it recognizes the bestial necessities and sanctifies them. By means of ritual it accompanies life with an apparatus which is essentially "worldly" and yet which, for anyone who has the spiritual capacity to transcend it, is full of mysterious and "superior" meaning, so that it reconciles its ceremonies with certain difficult aspirations of the

[1] From the title of a book by Mario Praz: *La Morte, la Carne, e il Diavolo* "Death, Flesh and the Devil." (*The Romantic Agony.*)

soul, and infuses into vital necessities a certain spirit which seems to transcend them and almost destroy their imperious reality.

April 15, 1937

There is appreciative taste and there is creative taste. I, who feel myself sufficiently gifted with the appreciative taste, am lacking in any creative capacity whatsoever; I would stop before ever even beginning any work. But there are so many excellent restorers who did not stop; Cavenaghi, for example. It is that restorers must and do know how to manage a paintbrush; so there is a great temptation to undertake personal work. Cavenaghi used to burn with impatience when he was restoring *The Last Supper* because he felt he was wasting time if he was not painting frescoes in a chapel which had been consigned to him. When at his insistence I finally went to see the frescoes myself, I could have wailed. There were absolutely no visible traces there of the genius of his taste. The tired Lombard tradition as we see it among the last followers of Procaccini, which would at least have been something sincerely felt and honest, had been bastardized by Cavenaghi with a view to impossible effects.

In general one can say that Italians think, feel, "live" artistically in a late sixteenth or seventeenth century style; so long as they are happy with it, everything goes well. Thus we see that the artisans are capable of renovating their work without breaking their schemes. They are not crystallized, but they continue to live their tradition, they love it, and they feel it to be contemporary. Today it is too late, but if even a hundred years ago artists had felt encouraged to respect what had always been their traditional spirit and ability, instead of letting foreign schemes and methods be imposed on them, eventually in that climate a painter of genius could have prospered and affirmed himself with a fully personal work, not the work of a disciple or a capricious "outlaw." Because there have been many, even among the recent Italian painters, who possess both talent and genius, but they have either borrowed their forms from other people, or they have found themselves standing too much alone, so the quality of their work is poor or false. One can see how much talent there is among the Italians who have been transplanted to Paris and who cannot be distinguished from the Parisians — who carry weight in Paris, and in fact in the whole sphere of modern painting: people like Boldini, De Nittis, Modigliani.

April 18, 1937

Weak or insecure people need a mythical figure through which they can feel represented and exalted.

"Official" Germany today is elaborating and imposing on its people the most stupid of religious (if we can bring ourselves to call them that) conceptions. It would be a clear, logical procedure (though it would grieve me a great deal) if "state policy" were to advocate a purely objective and positivistic vision of the world and of human destinies in opposition to religion, to the Christian "myth." But this return to Odin! A myth which is not even barbaric but only insipid, and which has no echoes in history but is completely buried in the consciousness of the people. We owe this to Wagner. If he had not "sung" the Nibelungs and imposed that legend on a whole people, we would not be able to speak about Odin today. But all the beer parlors, all the promenades, all the meetings, the societies, the homes, the love affairs of the Germans are pervaded by the waves of his music; everything is drowned by that musical tide which no longer allows anything different to float on it. Who knows how much longer the doors of the Church will be able to resist?

June 9, 1937

Sansovino carries the Renaissance to its extreme apex of perfection: the fusion and interpenetration of ornament and structure, the use of the most noble materials — marble, granite, bronze — and always a frugal use of them with no excesses; the adaptation of sculpture within the architectonic scheme without its being overdone, without its reaching gigantic, too-human proportions. It is the Renaissance which still excludes Michelangelo, which excludes any appearance of the subsequent Baroque. Here in Venice it is typified better than in any other place by the Logetta and by the Libreria of San Marco.

Tintoretto is not only or even primarily a man of genius and an "innovator." He is the painter who transferred everything onto a "heroic scale" with proportions which reconciled elegance and majesty in a manner that had never yet been seen. This *Last Supper* in San Trovaso could be called a "genre painting," a canvas inspired by the Flemish, and which fragment by fragment could be recognized in a Bassano; but it would be a Bassano which had by some miracle become heroic, a level which even Rembrandt never achieves. And when the genre piece — its manner, its virtuosity — are carried to this level, they become something entirely different; they are attributes of Tintoretto's heroic style; they almost underline it. There is something minute, precise, tiny, petty bourgeois, rustic I might even say, to "genre" in itself, which vanishes here altogether, resolving itself into the exact opposite. If anything, I am disturbed by that stimulus which Tintoretto was unable to resist, alongside his sense of the grandiose — a sort of spicy pimento which he puts everywhere, extremely elegantly. It is a temptation which continually dominates him. Intellectuals, as opposed to purely instinctive people, are often subject to the desire to illustrate, to a sense of "worldliness" which can reach the point of obscuring and even negating the essential austerity and sobriety of their art.

June 17, 1937

I would like to be, or would like to appear to be, different from what I am, but I have also learned to accept myself as I am and to recognize, in that strange and disconcerting individual who comes to meet me in the mirror at the end of the corridor, a being from whose company I will never be liberated except by suicide, because there is no divorce for cases of this kind, and I abhor that type of momentary divorce which drinking, or taking drugs, can provide. In the same way that I have learned to accept myself — and in fact more easily than with myself — I have learned to accept others, as being like flowers (when they are flowers) which blossom according to their own rule, not according to my will, and toward whom human relationships are finished if by some chance I do have to exercise my will on them, if I have to adopt them. True humanism is just this: to assist at the blossoming of flowers, to see men as aesthetic facts, as true works of art, laws unto themselves, alive through their own humanity; and not to impose oneself on them with one's own imagination and desires under the belying guise of exigency and moral paradigms.

June 19, 1937

In my new work[1] I am seeking to demonstrate that after any period of great artistic maturity there follows a period of impoverishment, of barbarization, of decadence, which always repeats the same forms of involution: the enlargement, stiffening and geometricization of contours. I am choosing the period which goes from the Emperor Hadrian to Giotto, but I could choose four or five others in the history of civilization, which all repeated the same precise formulas, and I could find indications of the same decadence outside of our Eurasian civilization among the African, Oceanic, Central-American artistic products. I do intend to refer to these other

[1] On the greatness and the decadence of art, to which Berenson applied himself for a long period, though it was never completed. Only one chapter of it appeared as a short book: *The Arch of Constantine, or The Decline of Form* (New York, Macmillan, 1955), but one can consider that Berenson's volume *Aesthetics and History in the Visual Arts* (New York, Pantheon, 1948) to some extent constitutes a general introduction to it.

diverse historical periods and countries in notes and com-
ments. A period of "decadence" does not mean that genius
is snuffed out; geniuses appear wherever they wish, they
make their voices heard in all periods and in the most pathological (decadent) ones they manifest themselves as a pa-
thetic recall, an almost shapeless promise of better times,
which is very captivating and subtle; this is what would be
called the "primitive genius." My center of interest is now
directed at a pathological age so my eye is open to all its
manifestations and I could study for hours some scribble
which would seem utterly futile to the eye of any expert who
was not impelled by the same motive that I am. My pleasure,
however, knows no limits of time and place; it is alive wherever there are the vibrations of genius (the extraordinary life
which I find in the frescoes of San Clemente in Rome, now
that I am studying them so closely, or in so many Byzantine
mosaics which are works of genius within one of the least rich
formulas known to us): without boasting I can say that I am
a free citizen in the kingdom of art. But precisely because
there was an accumulation and special intensity of genius in
certain periods, these are the ones in which I find the most
delight — they are my preferred areas: the Greek world for
ten centuries from the fifth century B.C. to the fifth century
A.D.; the Italian Renaissance from its dawn in 1400 to what
was really its true "age of gold" in 1550 — that brief period
which includes Raphael, Titian, Veronese, Tintoretto, and, let
us also add, Correggio. It was art's glory; it was the time of a
heroic, but not a distant vision of what was human, a time
of vivid yet peaceful sensuality, of voluptuousness which was

full of grace. After it the decadence was rapid. In this "history of artistic form" of mine I am most convinced by the fact that nothing is isolated in my imagination; there are no barriers either between the arts or between places, and I see historical civilization, the Euro-Asiatic world, as undergoing the same vicissitudes in all its manifestations. There are isopsychic lines as there are isothermic lines. Certain tendencies, certain specialized forms of research and of success, are repeated without knowing about each other, without influencing each other, from one corner to the other of this all-embracing realm of mine, with only brief, almost inadvertent differences of time; and there are the same echoes in different fields; Solon next to Socrates, Confucius almost contemporary with Buddha. The thing is that the civilization which we consider historical is a single whole, and is maturing at its various spatial points according to the same process of development.

The Victorian age, the last century, was also a great age — one which in the field of art is represented by French painting, from David to Degas — better still, to Matisse. It produced great inventiveness in all fields, in politics as well as in philosophy; and I see too that what is succeeding it in our days is very rapid decadence which is evidenced by bastardization and geometricization: everyone convinced by the beauty of geometry, everyone in raptures before rings and circles, before "non-objective art" as they like to call it in New York. This passion, which is both snobbish and genuine, on the part of the public gives me a glimpse of the raptures with which even the people most greatly endowed with taste

must have admired barbarian art objects when the last fires
of Alexandrian art had gone out and these people were already satiated by clumsy attempts produced out of the decadence of Rome.

June 20, 1937

The desire to touch is instinctive, from children to the
common man, almost as though experimenting with the resistance of objects were the only guarantee of their existence.
With art objects, with masterpieces, the same thing occurs:
whoever is most intellectually motivated, most expert, will
seek to "touch" through his imagination and ideas, to convince himself of the corporeality of objects by some other
means than pure touch. For the most proven admirers, "ideated sensations" substitute for the touch of the hand.

Nevertheless I feel sympathetic with anyone who does
touch, with anyone who does not keep himself from seeking
that immediate and "material" (if you wish to say it that
way) communication, because its materialness does have a
meaning, even if only embryonic, which so many abstruse
metaphysics and so many ideal assertions completely fail to
have. Contact is a desire for joining, love for the "thing in itself," of "itness" as I call it. And a work of art is, above all,
an irreplaceable, individual thing which knows nothing "beyond" itself, which is alone and essential in itself. Thus one
makes contact with art not theorizing or reading theories, but
looking, being in direct relationship. But since the work of art
is, from another standpoint, the living stone of the structure
in which we live, the most vivid incarnation of time, it is also

necessary to know this house where we live: our civilization, our history. And thus all the history which has already been explained, all historical works, help our knowledge of art, as does that other manifestation of life which is literature. My precept, better to say my admonition, is not to read works about the figurative arts, but to look, and then, with the greatest possible intelligence, comparative faculty, instinct, and education, to read (never enough) works of history and literature in order to always be putting the work of art into a more conscious relation with time, that is with the human element, and thus to be more successful in identifying, in deepening, the work of art in oneself.

June 22, 1937

Chateaubriand maintains a classical pose throughout his whole life, like that of a figure in a Poussin landscape.

July 4, 1937

It is not enough to have political intelligence; this is useful to the critics of politics. Politicians need a plastic sense of people, almost as though they were a ductile material in their hands.

The recent biography of Sargent, written by Charteris, is very insignificant. It is too bad, given that a book on Sargent could be quite important, since Sargent, more than anyone else, created the model and the pattern of a beauty which in the Anglo-Saxon countries lasted through the whole end of the nineteenth century and the beginning of this century.

This means that he stood at the center of an aesthetic mode, that he represented a cycle in taste, just as Raeburn and Gainsborough did in the eighteenth century, except that the latter was a more fertile time aesthetically. This is Sargent's major claim, but one must not forget that he is also a scrupulous observer, and that he is furnished with good instruments, a watchful eye, and a sure hand which always hits the target. So long as he did not become a courtier he also showed, in his portraits, a strong knowledge of character which was acute enough, in fact, to suggest caricature; and all this came through simple native ability; it was not conscious, since consciousness was lacking in him and he never really knew how to "organize." He is totally deprived of the gifts of imagination and composition; analogous in this to Cézanne, who was astounded whenever he saw a reproduction of an Italian painting of the Renaissance. But Cézanne is really a painter, with sovereign gifts, and even if he might have needed to have the entire painting, the typical and complete landscape, which he was reproducing, before his eyes, when he did reproduce it he penetrated and interpreted it to such an extent that his sea, hills and sky are of a quality which has never been seen before.

July 5, 1937

Moravia succeeds in giving a sense of a somber monochrome atmosphere in his stories. To me they always seem analagous to Victor Hugo's romantic drawings, all done in black shadows. As is true for so many people, his artistic personality, which is so monotonous and closed, seems to me to have only a very tenuous rapport with his real personality; like the neck of an hourglass. Writers (like painters) create their own form and are then slaves to it. When their form is so persistent, it becomes a manner, that is to say the easiest and sometimes indispensable means that they have at their command; and when the manner is accepted and pleasing to many, it becomes transformed into fashion. Fashion is nothing other than the easiest, most general, most persuasive form in any given period of time.

August 6, 1937

Kafka makes me think of the people about whom William James used to speak in my youth: they ooze convictions, but one fails to understand what the convictions are.

August 7, 1937

German art is pure Mediterranean art, but all superficialized, smoothed out, rounded out, so as to render it digestible to the Teutonic stomach.

August 11, 1937

The Arabs have no power of fantasy in their literature; the whole "bewitched" part of *The Arabian Nights* is not indigenous but is of Persiano-Indian origin. They have qualities of descriptive realism and qualities of poetic transfiguration, the qualities which one finds in English literature and which are the true artistic qualities in the long run — one cannot be abstracted from the other; together they form the essence of any work of art. But in the Arab lyrics (and descriptions) as in every other exotic art — Chinese, for example — a restricted world is being dealt with — sounds from only a few strings — and compared to the field of English art they add up to a paltry, extremely limited manifestation.

A book which I am reading now by Adama van Scheltema tries to prove that all "Nordic" art tends toward the abstract, toward pure combinations of lines, of planes, and of reliefs. And his demonstration is convincing, except that it proves something altogether different from what it meant to prove, which is that this is not art. Even the "Nordics" had a capacity for representation; it was just that they did not know how to do it, and the Mediterraneans were needed in order to enter the real kingdom of art, because they happily knew how to represent the human body.

August 19, 1937

The only interesting thing in the life of Shakespeare, except the fact of his birth and of having obtained genius from God (a genius which is like the meeting of two special, predestined beings who give birth to an exceptional son — his masterpieces) was that he had the possibility through Florio's lively translation, of encountering and immersing himself in the works of Montaigne. Very few critics, who spend all their time in worthless problems of identification and in filling out his biography with both documented and nonexistent facts, take any interest in this.

The mass of Shakespearian criticism is a consummate example of inconclusive criticism, and is a marvelous indication of the extent to which people flee from occupying themselves with a writer's art, and of how much they collect any pretext, the moment it presents itself, for going astray in tasks which allow them to hide their real objective from themselves.

Proust's manner of approaching others, and his appearance, were one of the most displeasing things possible. He acted like a real "rasta" in certain cases — a Rumanian Jew rather than a Parisian Jew. He had an absolutely oily timidity toward anyone who represented some "value" to him, whether worldly or cultural — toward anyone who from his point of view was in the ascendancy. To my misfortune I had been extolled to him by Lucien Henraux, with all the emphasis of the young when they are lyricizing the work of someone older than themselves, and then Proust had found information and inspiration in my books, so his encounters with me always left a false and boring impression on me.

August 20, 1937

The English language is an infinite sea with no shores; French is a sea which is full of enchanting islands, but also of perilous reefs.

December 1, 1937

Civilization is like the smoke of a locomotive: very beautiful and golden beneath the slanting rays of the sun, but in rainy weather simply something dirty and smelly. There is

certainly something which changes with the centuries: my-
thologies change, and this means a great deal, if man is essentially, as the philosopher used to say, "a creator of divinity."

December 4, 1937
   Values are by necessity a religious matter; there is nothing
to demonstrate them or recommend them, but it is on them
that we ground ourselves; whether or not they be accompanied by a mythology is of relatively little importance.

   Why does English lend itself so well to translation? Because it is a language which is not restricted by grammatical
usage but is "in process of Becoming" — modifiable at every
step; and also it includes two complete and distinct vocabularies: the Teutonic and the Latin, with appreciable but delicate differences in the usages and thus great richness of overtones. It is the same reason that makes English poetry so
special. German is also a language inured to and fit for
translations, but less so than English, not because of the
shades of tone in English vocabulary, but because English
possesses many "keys" in its construction, many turns of
phrase which never smack of the bizarre, so it is adaptable
to different lines.

   The tactile values (the sense of form) are essential to the
figurative arts. Other highly "spiritual" qualities cannot take
precedence over them. For line to communicate a sense of refinement, of delicacy, it always has to be at the same time a
functional, not calligraphic line — one which comprehends

and indicates plasticity with the same vigorousness that a model would. The line which is simply a flat detail does not define anything, and has a purely ornamental value. In Byzantine art, in Sienese art, there is a sort of confusion of the two values, or a transition from the lowest to the highest, without the former ever entirely disappearing. But where the "spiritual values" are best affirmed (in Duccio, in Simone Martini) there is certainly no negation of functionality; there is something already very alive and molded in the figures despite, and really reinforcing, their linear elegance — something without which they would say nothing to us; but because they lack perfect sureness of form there does remain some residue of ornamentality.

December 5, 1937

Matisse is a magnificent draftsman, but he has never seemed to me to be a good colorist. His paintings are attuned to pink, as though he worked *à jour* on a pink substratum, indicating the rest of the colors only as shadows. And his pink is a pallid, cheap color; it gives a sense of aridity rather than richness.

December 7, 1937

The construction, the technique of *Salammbô* has always made me think of Paolo Uccello's battle scenes: lifeless horses stuffed with straw, warriors in petrified poses. One feels a lack of internal force in Flaubert — a lack of "value" —value in the sense of the profound conviction that moves one to write. Werfel on the other hand does possess the vital

mystical élan which in his work is always somehow subdued
— never excessive. The sense of value is in fact a mystical
sense; and whoever does not incarnate this value in something, but feels it in its own terms or at the very most pin-
pointed in a mythology, should properly be called mystical.

Among the various forms of memory there exists a "professional memory" which has the hardest time dying. Mine
is helped by the fact that essentially it does not lean on words
and concepts, but on illustrations. Any article which I read
and which is important to me to remember is always accompanied by illustrations, and these, as soon as I have seen them,
remain in my mind together with the captions which describe them and which succinctly indicate the meaning and
the importance of the article; in this way my task is greatly
facilitated. All I have to do is to make a note of the article,
and this functions as the item of an index.

December 10, 1937
Dali has taken whatever pieces from Tura and from Cossa
are the most contorted and the most pointedly marked; he has
placed them upside down together with the most incongruous
things, and in this way has created an art for himself which
simpletons admire highly. In all probability he has acted
with total cynicism. His forerunners, notably someone like
Picasso, had great qualities as draftsmen; their technique
was masterful and flexible. One cannot really tell if Dali possesses this, or if he is simply a manipulator of puzzles.

Mysticism is not a form of knowledge because knowledge is always about something, and mysticism, on the contrary, is immediacy, central experience.

December 16, 1937

Few people are good, just as few people are artists. But the admiration of goodness, which is no mean thing, can be expected from everyone, just as it is possible for everyone to recognize and admire art.

December 17, 1937

Many people possess convictions only insofar as they are not capable of reflecting on the things about which they are convinced.

December 19, 1937

By this time churches are full of images and objects which represent the negation of art, which cry out the absence of any artistic sincerity: they are full of so-called "bondieuserie." For a century, from 1820 on, one may say, there has been no more religious art — a patent proclamation of the lack of real faith. Where, and in whom, is faith manifested today? It is difficult to say. There exists a manifestation of rudimentary, paleochristian faith which is commonly called Communism, or Bolshevism, and which is not an appetite for welfare, as the reactionaries say, but is a true faith which exalts men's spirits and pushes them to sacrifice. There exist those of us, a few remnants, who profess humanism, and whom the Communist faith runs up against not in interests but on account of its own extremist, iconoclastic force — the "icons" which it wants to destroy being in fact the values which we hold most precious. Whether conscious or illusory, there exist violent people who oppose faith in the name of nothing more than an outlet — who believe only in force, and worship it as a possibility for exploiting the weak and defenseless.

December 21, 1937

Salammbô is like an eternal turtle soup, which sticks to one's lips. It is reading matter which one cannot follow for any length of time without becoming nauseated. *Bouvard et Pécuchet* is the epic of banality; maybe it is a book which does not stand on its own because it is inspired by nothing but disgust, by disgust for the very instrument itself of the writer, that is, for the human mind, and this is disgust on which nothing — not even a true and proper satire — can be built.

"Odium facit versus." It is not true. Hate is something arid and prolonged, a mode of being and of living of the same genre as vengeance, a dish of food which is always eaten cold. In indignation, on the other hand, which is a rapid, generous, and quickly extinguished emotion, there exist warmth, vitality, and, though perhaps by contrast, creative virtue. I am afraid of hatred; it is a state of the soul in which I feel myself annihilated, as though all nobility were taken from me and thereby also all capacity to conceive, but indignation can be everyday fare — a ready and vital form of reaction.

Dreiser and Conrad are two contrasting cases: Dreiser being the lively genius with no talent, incapable of using his instrument, essentially ignorant of his own craft; and Conrad, lacking in genius but provided with a portentous talent for creating "ex novo," almost "ex nihilo," a means of expression which is imposed on the reader and convinces him of improbable situations and characters all filled with shadowiness and leaks. Dreiser's concept of "tragedy" is perfect: a book in which there is no escape, not one moment to draw breath, everything compact and ineluctable; but nonetheless it is strangely unformed. Conrad, on the other hand, conducts his oblique situations with mastery; he creates an almost sensual romanticism which justifies any lack of balance in the characters, and he works as if by verbal magic.

January 14, 1938

Symbols acquire vogue in rough, primitive times, and in times of decadence they are a symptom and a product of mental fatigue, both from exhaustion, and from maturity not yet achieved or richness not yet accumulated. When art is in full bloom it does not know what to do with symbolism. It doesn't have to point out or copy anything; it expresses directly. What serves art is metaphor, that is, the image, which is never a symbol but an artistic reality, an immediate manner of seeing.

January 15, 1938

Americans are free, independent beings who all spasmodically tend to identify themselves with a single type: whichever type arouses the greatest success among them.

All woven into English poetry are golden, or purple, or azure threads — these being the allusions to other works by their own poets, to mythology, and to classical literature. Only two poets are immune from it: Blake and Burns. Reading all the others presupposes a humanistic substratum which is the common patrimony of our average culture. But this explains the difficulty of interpreting Chinese poetry and why Waley had to forego the translation of a number of poems which to us, in our ignorance of Chinese culture, would have been absolutely incomprehensible. Any Chinese translation of English poetry would be equally obscure.

January 16, 1938
Each time I have ever formulated a theory, my first thought the following morning has been to cast it aside. Most men formulate theories and then stay prisoners of them both in life and in death.

January 18, 1938
Tennyson was essentially the poet of the middle, or the upper middle class. He led the good Victorian burghers along an easy flat road to a lofty place which they would not have known how to reach on their own, but which conformed to them in every way, without any surprises or dizzy heights.

William Morris is a tapestry painter in his poetry. His visions have that remote, fairy-tale tone of voice — those tenuous nuances which are properly characteristic of tapestries.

T. S. Eliot's poetry? It does not exist, unless transformed into mere literature. His is a literary effort, like that of the fifth century Latin poets. I don't say that he is a plagiarist, but he is a poet of medleys. This mania for echoes and repetitions, for combinations derived from various sources, is so rooted in him that he is no longer aware that he is imitating, and he moves in artificial air as though it were pure air.

The central motif of his poetry is great abstinence; in this he is clearly American — the typical puritan who believes that salvation may only be obtained by dint of denial, and first and foremost aesthetic denial. This is the "punctum dolens" of Eliot, and is what makes me indignant. Among artists, he is the most decadent, since he renounces and blasphemes his own instrument, like someone who renounces his own mother. Very few Indian things truly please me, but one does to an extraordinary degree: the "punja," the prayer which every Indian peasant recites each morning in front of his spade or hoe before beginning his work. Such adoration of one's own instrument is a beautiful thing, and renders men worthy of whatever work they achieve. It is the precise opposite of Eliot's attitude.

To me the most unsupportable dandy is the intellectual dandy; the man who carries his own minuscule, new interpretation, his own microscopic discovery, in his buttonhole like a gardenia.

The cinema, according to me, stands in relation to the theater as the theater does to sculpture; or like an express train in relation to a man's step. It is the theater carried to the point of a vertiginous race, and thus to complete passivity on the part of the spectator, who becomes like a traveler setting out in an automobile at one hundred kilometers an hour who cannot enjoy anything of the landscape except as a series of images moving in quick succession which no longer ask of him that he make any effort either of attention or of persistence. It puts people in the habit of a sequence of emotions which permits of no interpretation, which is lashed by time. It is not like music, in which time is transfigured as harmony, because it must lean on well-known illustrations, on a description. We know that descriptive music is a counterfeit of music, precisely because it is no longer uniquely itself. Couldn't cinematography be considered a composition of lights, a harmony of scenic sequences? We must return to what I was saying first — to elements which even in the "fixed" arts, so to speak, are recognized as theatrical, and therefore decadent. I do not wish to say that the theater may not have a sort of office and that it not be in some way artistic; but it is not (insofar as it is spectacle) true art; cinematography even less so. And this is without taking into account the exaggerations of its monotony today, and its abuse of emotive expression, which is now like a school for physical poses, not a source of artistic excitement.

January 27, 1938

In general, art criticism is completely useless work — commercial and heterogeneous. The critic ought to do only one thing: tell us which works are beautiful, unless he can attempt a work of art on his own — pouring off his aesthetic enjoyment into words and images. Whoever seeks the path of artistic understanding in criticism hits a false road; he finds there only a surrogate which serves no purpose except to remove him from real experience and to render him obtuse. A work of art is like women: "il faut coucher avec." The fewer books one reads, the readier one will become for immediate experience, for contact with the art in itself, for ecstasy (ek-stasis). Getting out of oneself, forgetting everything, in order to "be" that extraordinary and yet so natural thing which is the work of art.

January 30, 1938

Renoir derived inspiration for his paintings from the most everyday reality, and we continually find his "types" in the streets and public squares. But the most everyday reality is never made up of skeins of many-colored wool like Renoir's pictorial material.

January 31, 1938

The Renaissance was an essentially anthropomorphic period; the occupation and preoccupation of man dominated in all the fields of the spirit, and particularly in art, where anatomy, as a study, reached a high degree of perfection. Artists then used to study the human body and understood it intelligently. They availed themselves of the experience of muscular movements, of walking, which every man possesses, and they amplified this experience by assisting themselves, together with drawing, with mannikins which they made assume all sorts of poses and movements. In this way they cultivated their muscular imagination, and could "invent" and surprise bodies in the most varied and daring positions and actions, presenting and foreseeing effects and results which would be reached much later when practical experience had become better developed — for example with the Russian ballet. In this imagination of theirs they were capable of exaggeration, perhaps, but never of error, since it was not born "out of the void," so to speak, but was the product of an intuition which lay close to science. Muscular imagination is one of the essential elements of art, as are the tactile values. And perhaps this sort of diligent imagination, which imagines things that are possibilities and that are always new, is one of the most important aspects of art, which is always a "continuation of nature."

(This is the abstract of a conversation held with Igor Markevitch and his first wife, Nijinsky's daughter.)

February 3, 1938

Memory is similar to a chain. And beware if any links are missing! If its duration cannot be traced right back to the beginning; if there is a vacuum in the middle, one feels a great sense of pain, a true desperation.

February 4, 1938

Life is like a tower; first one becomes used to the highest floor, and then little by little one descends, from floor to floor, not because anything serious happens, but simply because the years pass. One has, each time, a sense of debasement; one finds oneself at another level, one realizes that things have changed and that the horizon has shrunk; and then finally one is reduced to the ground.

February 5, 1938

Sensitivity only for modern art: that would be like talking about someone who was able to smell vinegar and taste garlic.

Holman Hunt's painting is made up of countless stamps, stuck on one next to the other.

February 6, 1938

I rebel at the qualification: "masters of self-expression" for the very modern painters. They are definable precisely by the fact that they do not express anything of their own, but follow whatever expression is indicated by the fashion, by the masses, by a desire for novelty and strangeness which is diffused through and easily accepted by the multitudes (even when they are still the snobbish multitudes and not the popular masses) precisely because it does not correspond to anything personal or intimate. Dali a self-expressive artist? Dali is a good draftsman who has set himself to drawing the incongruous in order to please certain currents, to appease certain extra-artistic theories which are mental phenomena, anything but artistically personal. The incongruous is not the expression of an artistic value, because it goes back into the field of cognition. "Painting of the incongruous" has therefore, if anything, programmatic value, like cubism and abstract painting; or "spy" value, in denoting the tiredness of obvious academicism, of normality when it is transmuted into conventionality. But the normal is not conventional; it is simply not pathological. And the incongruous incontestably postulates the congruous; in a certain sense its triumph (if one can call it that) denotes an imminent return to the normal state; it is attractive precisely because it sets itself up in opposition to an imminent normal state. If the incongruous were to become the norm of our days, it would have no attraction for anybody.

In the abnormal there is no manifestation of personality, for it would be too easy a way of manifesting it. What then is the "norm" if not the best condition for human life, and thereby also the best for art? It is not a dogma but the result of a human experience, and cannot be challenged by caprice, taste, or games without there being a loss of human qualities. The incongruous seems to be self-expressive, the way a blow in the eye might be; but all blows are similar whereas true artistic manifestations are not, even when they adopt infantile, stammering language because of technical inexperience or the low level of the times.

Mannerisms are quite another thing; mannerisms are expressive — perhaps too easily, indulgently expressive — of a certain elegance, of a certain accentuation which can also be synonymous with badly channeled energy. Look at Parmigianino or El Greco, and all the Byzantine hieratics before him.

Is there any true painter whom one can say lacks feeling? Certainly not: and Piero della Francesca, whom I have defined as impassive, is not just a painter of pure things, and figures, and spaces, and lines, and expanses of color. Those figures of his are laden with energy, with something which comes from a far distance and gazes into a far distance. The Christ of the *Resurrection* is entirely imbued with this force. When one says "sentimentality" one wants to denounce a sentiment in which one is no longer participating; not that there may not be purely illustrative painting — vignettes and "keepsakes" — but that is no longer painting. When we say for example that Millet is sentimental it simply means we are reacting against a sentiment which is no longer fashionable, and because of that reaction we forget to appreciate the value of Millet's paintings: solid, noble painting which ranks with the best of the nineteenth century. Naturally Van Gogh, whose way of painting, furthermore, is influenced by Millet, especially by Millet's drawings, is not considered sentimental by his admirers. Now his is really one of the more shameful sentimentalities — sentiment which possesses him with such fury as to reduce him to madness. His painting is the enraged denunciation of a man of the proletariat, of a malcontent. However, it has value, because it is moved by that force, but one should not call it impassive, or "pure painting." It will now no longer be understood as a peroration of violence, because Van Gogh's denunciatory violence is no more noticed, and it does not offend in the way that the elementary quality of Millet's sentiment offends precisely because of the degree to which it is elementary. It is so much closer to a "norm" of sentiment that it will undoubtedly come back into predominance and be accepted. Van Gogh is pleasing because his calligraphy is very clear and everyone can follow it on the canvas, so people delude themselves, as they look at his work, into thinking they are becoming one with a technique — as though this were something important to art and as though the great masters had no "technique." In their work it is secret and almost eclipsed; it is much less easy to get at it and trace it.

February 8, 1938

I wish that no one, in the field of the figurative arts, would busy themselves with attributions. This is a preparatory philological work which has had to be done, in the same way that three hundred years ago for example, a Homeric dictionary had to be compiled. Nobody today needs to rewrite a Homeric dictionary any longer in order to read the *Iliad;* everyone has the good fortune to be able to work with the one which has already been done. The game and the curiosity of compiling directories of works of art does not matter anymore; what is important is finding the essential elements in them — what I would call the "curves" or parabolas of art, which mean, certainly, the artistic personalities of the painters or sculptors, but not at all in the personal sense. The historical individual does not interest us at all. A parabola of art, one moment of art, can comprehend diverse individuals — this is the lesson which I have tried to give with the "Amico di Sandro" — while on the other hand one same historical individual can belong to two different parabolas. I would like it if nobody even knew the names of the individuals (names are a historical accident) and if each parabola were considered by itself, without vocabularies to designate it.

It lives in and of itself. The individual accident — the historical personality of the artist — adopts it as it is and cannot, through will, make it oscillate by a millimeter.

Nature is a magnificent deposit of sensations.

February 11, 1938

In my youth I was seized by a real passion for medieval Latin poetry. And perhaps it was through the "pastiches" of medieval Latin that I approached Baudelaire for the first time. Certainly it was the easiest Latin to read, but this was not the only thing which induced me to read it and then to become so enthusiastic about it. I am always attracted by hymns, by ritual in literature, by the incantation of words which are repeated and almost sung chorally. I found the same literary pomp and ceremony transposed in Byzantine mosaics, which from then on I undertook to study as much as I could.

June 11, 1938

Donatello is the Rembrandt of sculpture; in his works there are nervous details, plays of shadow; there is not the clear, sober, powerful structure of the young Luca della Robbia, before his famous (all too famous) glazed terracottas, for instance the little bas-relief in the Bargello: a perfect parallel to Masaccio's painting.

June 19, 1938

German writers who are certainly fully sincere, cannot clearly put forth simple ideas, because if they were to do this it would seem to them that they did not have enough "profundity," and in order to be profound they complicate everything to the point of absurdity. So Kantorowicz is already hard enough to read, but no one is comparable to Srbik: *Deutsche Einheit*. His book is like a pie made of several layers of thorns interlaced in various ways. It is stuff which is not only indigestible, but absolutely unchewable.

June 22, 1938

Snobbishness is the gods' gift for facilitating the education of the populace.

June 28, 1938

Andrea del Castagno is one of those painters toward whom my attitude always used to be best expressed by a paraphrase of the Biblical words: "God, I like it; help my unliking it." Now I have arrived at the point of knowing why I cannot like it. He is too expressionistic, he poses his figures too cinematographically, he is too far from that "essential construction" which to Burckhardt was the peak of art.

August 9, 1938

English literature would never have been born without the classics. They are like blue veins running all through it, alive under the skin.

When I landed in America, and reporters were begging me to give them some information about myself, I told them:

"My career is well known enough, my works are written, and anyone can read them; all the rest — my thoughts, my life — is purely accidental and is of no interest to anybody." They went off quite satisfied to put these words of mine into print.

August 11, 1938

Photography is an artistic instrument, like the paintbrush — but it is an instrument whose application is more restricted and circumscribed. One can, with photography, achieve effects similar to Chinese art, not effects similar to the great Italian art.

August 13, 1938

Many American women possess nine parts of energy to one single part of intelligence.

August 14, 1938

Neophytes, particularly the American ones, catch Catholicism the way savages do syphilis: with a tremendous violence.

Malta, like Venice, is entirely a stone landscape. The houses are old stones, the earth is stone, and even the isolated trees are stone, or, if not stone, jade.

August 16, 1938

The French types whom I cannot stand are those who appear to have been born in Rumania. A memorable example is Boni de Castellane.

The "Sapphic" reputation of Sappho is owed to the malignity of the Greeks. Sappho was nothing but an excellent seminar director who established the scope of her life as being to illuminate her pupils, so the day that one did not stay to listen to her, she threw herself into the sea in disillusionment.

August 19, 1938

A landscape with no history seems to me like a house with no books.

August 21, 1938

"Homo vivit in paucis," says the Latin poet. This is the tragedy of humanity at the present time, that it has apprehended all the inhuman products of the mind without leaving any more room for the human. The maximum of what is "human" is the universal conscience in man; this living form of egocentricity, of anthropocentricity, which each of us — but we are very few — can experience. The physical, mechanical sciences and practical discoveries have eaten up the whole field of knowledge; what is lacking is a parallel process, not so much in the moral sciences as in the "religio" which teaches men and indicates to them what makes life worthwhile. Today the "religio" of the young lies in speed. But so long as "humanitas," this higher conscience, endures even in very few people, our minds can be at ease; the "point d'appui," the springboard remains, from which the many can be made to feel it — or there still remains at least the hope that this can come to pass.

D'Annunzio only "posed" if there were a group of people gathered together, but Duse "posed" even in conversation with a single person.

For D'Annunzio words were like those precious stones in barbarian jewelry which are mounted on a shapeless, artistically worthless object, simply for the pleasure of their glitter.

August 22, 1938

The Bible is the single, grandiose document which remains to us of a land-bound people, people from the hinterland, which resisted and asserted itself against the invasion of a navigating people, the Philistines. It is as though we had had an epic era of Samnites, or ancient Latins, preceding the Etruscan invasions, or an epic era of the aboriginal Italiots before the colonies of Magna Grecia. The ancient civilizations of the Etruscans, Cretans, Phoenicians, Greeks all came and spread themselves by way of the sea, dominating and annihilating the previous landed civilizations with the power and industriousness of their new methods of conquest. Only the Israelites resisted, with an extraordinary manifestation of spiritual force, and if ever they submitted, it was only materially, without their strength being extinguished.

August 25, 1938

The beasts in the caves of Altamira are pure representation; art certainly, but in the sense and the manner that the song of a bird is art. I feel I must make a great difference between art in such an immediate and primitive sense as this, and the historical, classical, reflective art which began with the first Egyptian dynasties and, to a parallel extent, with Babylon. Knossos is the protracted manifestation and the blossom of unreflective art; it is art which is not yet conscious of its own traditions but comes close to geometric formulas, that is to a scheme, from which conscious art will flower. And I mean by that conscious art any art which concentrates essentially, and from the beginning, on the nude. I have not yet formulated the distinction between the two arts, the transition from the unreflective to the reflective worlds, in any way which satisfies me, but I have had an intuition about it for a long time — I would say for more than twenty years. I still remember having discussed it with Eugénie Strong,[1] and I remember her owl eyes as she listened to me talk, eyes which she always makes when she understands nothing of what is being said to her, but knows it is about a subject which ought to interest her. In any case I think that classical art has lasted from Egypt to the present day, but that there are always cases of people or primitive individuals who manifest themselves in art with a spontaneity which is over and above any tradition.

November 3, 1938

Dante is like a revolving dovecote, with so many holes and compartments in which one can find and put anything and everything one wants.

---

[1] Mrs. Arthur Strong, from 1909 to 1925 assistant director at the British School in Rome.

November 6, 1938

It was Varus' fault that he let himself be beaten by Arminius. If Varus had won and Rome had succeeded in dominating all of Germany, Germany would have become wholeheartedly Mediterranean, without reservations and without discontent in relation to the civilization of Europe. Another fault, or another misfortune, lay in the fact that Rome did not conquer central Arabia; if this had happened history would never have known the Mohammedan incursions. Subsequently Germany, in her turn, would have done better to turn toward Russia, for there, however half barbaric she might have been, she would have been able to perpetrate a civilizing effect. Three shameful historical events of which we are now paying the consequences.

For me civilization consists of the more and more complete humanization of man, and despite all the uprisings, and the obstacles, this does go on, following a zigzag, uncertain path, with heights and depths, like a temperature graph wherein the average level, however unnoticeably it may be, is rising.

November 7, 1938

German art has been expressionistic from the time of the Ottos. Naumburg and Meissen are examples of the full bloom of expressionism: those numbed, contorted movements of the bodies, those faces which are not content with repeating the same movements but exaggerate them even more, to the point where pathos is associated with a grim-

ace. So much of modern art can be found therein, "in nuce."
In order for artistic expression to be pure and classical, it
should not be physiognomic, but should be contained in the
lines of the bodies themselves, without therefore exaggerat-
ing them to the extent of a sort of exasperated hieroglyphic.
As I have said at other times, I would enjoy a population of
statues with no heads . . .

November 8, 1938

It is a secondary matter for me that Piero should have
been a master of perspective and should have opened up a
new path, new horizons, in pictorial technique. What is important to me is the "vis a tergo" which pushes him, which
inspires him with enthusiasm, and which makes him reach
those perfect results toward which technique is simply a
means. It is his total, grandiose, heroic vision — so powerful and overwhelming — which could do no less than find a
suitable means of expression and which naturally had at its
command, within its domain, a "technique."

Cézanne is the last and conclusive master of a tradition
(after him it is shattered). It is still the tradition of Piero
della Francesca, taken in a certain sense from Piero, and in
fact I am convinced that Piero had a knowledge of ancient
painting which is lost to us but which acted like a fertilizer
for his genius. Cézanne represents that same tradition almost totally transferred to landscape, with his absolutely
cubic values of plastic forms affirming themselves in a way
which never occurred before, and values of "form" being

transferred from the country to the sky, which until then had been the background and scenario of paintings. Cézanne incorporates the sky with the earth; it forms part of a whole, and is the live interior of a solid.

My books are too brief and epigrammatic, and for this reason they have often been completely misunderstood. I remember one anecdote: Solomon Reinach was full of enthusiasm for my *Florentine Painters,* in which I speak of tactile values; one day, rather mysteriously, he drew my wife aside and said: "Dites donc, ces choses que votre mari a écrites, est-ce que vous croyez qu'on peut les expliquer aux jeunes filles?" [1]

November 13, 1938

The artist is (or especially was) only conscious of his technique; unconscious of his genius, which is like the "vis a tergo" of his work. Preconceived ideals, religious aspirations, are irrelevant matters; he is a technician who has learned from a master, who has thus found and appropriated a certain series of forms and models, and who develops them or modifies them according to an impulse which is, precisely, his genius, or his inspiration, and this is not something external to the work of art — not a program. The only program the artist used to know was the one imposed on him by whoever commissioned him, and he accepted it voluntarily; that is, he did not even discuss it. Only a rebel like

---

[1] "Tell me now, about these things which your husband has written — Do you think one can explain them to young girls?"

Michelangelo was able to oppose it, and, in fact, he is the only one among the great artists of the past who, from the beginning, "created" (as a modern, post-romantic artist would do) according to personal "ideas."

November 16, 1938

Jane Austen is to Dickens as Vermeer is to Rembrandt. They are incomparable — Dickens truly possesses the greatness and all the weaknesses of Rembrandt, but a humorist has no parallel in painting, except in caricature, which is too facile and clumsy a form.

I have always taken exception to the theater's too strongly emotive faculty. I am so easily excitable that for me a theatrical spectacle always sins through excess, and lacks sobriety and economy. I remember when, as a child, I went to the theater for the first time; after the first act I no longer understood anything anymore; everything, the audience, the stage, whirled around me, because I was so consumed by my effort of attention and by the intensity of my impressions.

November 19, 1938

O'Neill's characters are like human buoys: they are bloated, exaggerated figures tossed around on stormy waves.

The great painting of the Italian Renaissance comprises no works which bear the stamp of the "studio." I mean works where one sees objects and forms, colors and shades, "studied," mannikins, and masks, color and virtuosity pieces, with the disorder, or false order which all those things possess in the studio of a painter. Technique, finally, is reabsorbed in them. Not so in Rembrandt. The young Rembrandt is almost always a "studio" painter; and often the more mature Rembrandt is too. He is, many times, a painters' painter, because they pay most attention to the detail and to virtuosity, and when they make a criticism they criticize technique, which is something very different from art criticism.

November 22, 1938

Frankly popular, peasant art, which lasts, or has lasted until a little while ago from Sweden to Rumania, from the Tyrol to Ireland, is a translation and a provincial perpetuation of Romanesque art. Like the latter it has a very lively sense of color and of the harmony of colors. It is a pre-Gothic art, of the thirteenth century. The Gothic has always obscured that negative and unexpected sense of harmony, and today one finds it in the most remote corners.

January 15, 1939

"Homo homini lupus." But what would women be for women if they were left to themselves? Hyenas.

January 16, 1939

The lyricism of Goethe (in the second *Faust,* for example) is all an aerial rhythm without any need of realistic significance, and which anticipates Shelley; every so often there is a solid block of gnomic reality in those dizzy heights and

vortices. The rhythm of this Goethe is comparable, like that
of Shelley, to the rhythm of Botticelli. It is most staggering
to point out that Shelley could not have known Goethe; it
means that quite independently from one another, two similar poetic innovators came to light at that time.

January 26, 1939
  Realists represent objects as the human race saw them
forty years earlier.

  I have been attracted by the expansive strength of Catholicism; and it is that quality in it which rises above and in a
certain sense contradicts the strict Thomistic system. Thomistic philosophy has always seemed to me to be something
closed, locked, like a game of Chinese boxes, and in Dante's
universe, for example, I have never been able to breathe,
though I have admired it from outside, aesthetically, as
something complete and perfect even down to its minute
details. Perhaps it is because an Anglo-Saxon upbringing
has made me restive about the spirit of systems, about all
philosophic systems except, at one time, the Platonic, which
is the one in which the most air circulates. According to me,
in order to live there is always a need for impulses and pro-
pulsions, for a medium which expands, instead of a compact
and constricted air, a need for that which feeds and enlivens logic instead of a universal geometry of fixed schematic
proportions. That food and that expression are at home in
Catholicism, and I have even felt them most strongly in
Catholicism. I shall never forget that experience.

No historian can get out of his own time, in the same way that no one can elude the laws of gravity. One can go up in an airplane or a balloon, but no matter how much one removes oneself from the earth's crust the law of gravity always dominates. Thus one can hover on high, one can dominate one's own time and one's own conditions, but one can never detach oneself from them to transfer oneself into a different time; the higher one goes the more one is able to see far-distant times from an advantageous position, but the position will always be ours, and tied to that which ties us.

April 15, 1939

Men consist of a mass of energy which pretty closely follows a certain tendency — which follows a road similar to the highways of Asia Minor, those roads which every so often disappear but come out again farther along in the same direction.

Mental power is a power of coördination between ideas and impulses. Straight logic is an inhuman activity, "Combinans in vacuo." Logic gets applied to certain premises which are the richness and reserve of human nature.

April 20, 1939

In my day one plucked the "flower" of education from a certain type of feminine and familial education which gave women a domestic, reserved tone, but not one which was at

all extraneous to life. It was an education which was immune from the "communal" or college spirit, but it was not
a servant's education either. Girls who were brought up in
that way knew how to adapt themselves well to worldly matters without fears and without timidities, and furthermore
they brought an intact internal purity to their rapports with
the world — a detachment which was neither severe nor
haughty; I would say it was something "saintly," but it
had nothing puritanical to it. It was an education which
stemmed from a perfect sense of individual sovereignty, that
is, from the sense, which once was feudal, that there is no
necessity nor reason to fraternize, and that it is in the family,
above all in a numerous and united family — as varied and
sufficient unto itself as they used to be — that one finds the
measure of all things. That sense of oligarchal feudal liberty is getting lost, and yet now is the time, since the feudal
barriers have been broken, that it could be extended to all
individuals who respected and nurtured in themselves their
power as individuals instead of the power of the mass. In a
parallel fashion the myth of "experience" has been growing.
Even people who could act differently have wanted to im-
part an education to the young which takes care of the "experience of life." But experience is the easiest thing to avail
oneself of, if one has a gift for it — and without that internal
gift, without the innate capacity for exploiting experience,
it is of no use for anything. The girls whom I remember
made a treasure of everything, because they were instinctively gifted; they were never lost and inquisitive in front of
things. Today education is the prerogative of the state, of

the colleges, of the masses, and that perfection which I have in mind will never appear again.

April 21, 1939

Through a natural habit of introspection I am aware of my own body even when I am not sick; I seem to feel it the way a swimmer would feel the different temperatures of water if he were to pass from a tub of boiling water, to cold water, and then again into tepid water, through all the possible variations, for a quarter of an hour at a time.

I was six or seven years old when I "heard" silence (I later learned it was the pulsing of my own blood, filling the absolute silence). At that time I was writing childish verses, and as though it were the most natural thing in the world I began a poem as follows: "Ringing silence is swimming all around."

April 23, 1939

Since England did not have a past which was rich in vital elements and institutions, it is the country where feudalism, introduced as a perfectly ideated and coherent "system" by William the Conqueror, was able to blossom and survive right down to our own day. Feudalism is the tree on which all the English liberties have grown through the centuries. Another country of full, unsullied feudalism was Latin Jerusalem, with the institution of its "assizes." But in that case the Moslem world which surrounded it cut off its development and its life after just a few decades.

April 29, 1939

More than thirty years ago a very elegant Russian whom I knew and who for certain of his strangenesses and refinements sometimes amused me, came to find me one morning and begged me to accompany him to the Uffizi at all costs. Once we were there, he rushed with me to Simone Martini's *Annunciation* and there he expressed all his disgust, all his horror for that painting, because, he said, "I cannot stand Annunciations in which the angel is not flying." That for me is the symbolic pose of the intellectual dandy: of the man, that is, who creates purely arbitrary values — or non-values — for himself with the purpose of being an eccentric, and who seeks salvation through exclusion.

Saint Thomas was the infinitely greater and better Herbert Spencer of his time — times which were incomparably aristocratic and subtle in relation to those of Spencer.

August 21, 1939

The modernists wanted something absurd and contradictory in terms: they wanted to rationalize Catholic dogma. It would be like wanting to derationalize mathematics.

December 8, 1939

America is really America only in its solitudes and free, open spaces. New York is the baroque gateway to an unknown land.

Magicians disturb me. They don't have anything to do with any cosmic order, which is what I prefer — an order where reason tries desperately to live against adverse and brutal forces.

December 14, 1939

The third page of the *Osservatore Romano* portrays a magic world enclosed in a stinking sacristy.

January 22, 1940

When one assists at the beginnings of a movement which seems subversive, or, worse, seems born out of the most base and bestial instincts of human nature, one must never despair. The first appearance of Christianity announces a complete destruction of whatever culture and spiritual delicacy there then was in the world. It was incomprehensible barbarism as far as the spirits and customs of a Roman or Hellene were concerned, and yet the Christian movement imposed itself, and by imposing itself has channeled and saved everything which it was able to transmit to the future of the ancient civilization. There is an immense diversity which runs from the word of Christ to the first apostolic Christianity, and from this to the "Christianity" known in the last centuries, — that diversity being entirely filled by the process of history.

January 24, 1940

The "nasalness" of American Yankee pronunciation — of the pronunciation, that is, of the pure descendants of the

first inhabitants of New England — is a relic of ecclesiastical chant which was diffused in a community where the custom was confused with Puritan theocracy, and where it had arrived by way of a popular tradition of "Lollards" from time immemorial, in fact right from the cantors of the synagogue (for whom singing through the nose was a form of respect to the divinity). The steady and ecclesiastical chant which is used today in the Catholic Church and in the "highest" Protestant churches is, by contrast, a courtly and Hellenic tradition, revived again by the Renaissance as a very cultured form of veneration, and thus restricted to the "closed" clergy and to the most organic hierarchies.

January 25, 1940

Bülow was the typical frivolous and elegant German who with earnestness and ponderousness treated serious matters frivolously: a type whose only terrain for blossoming and acquiring political power is at court. It is a type which I have never found sympathetic; the only Germans for whom I have ever felt any inclination are the solid Germans, and I don't mean to say the heavy Germans.

The Greeks loved life so ardently that their admiration for anyone who was able to sacrifice it knew no bounds. Thus Homer exalted heroism in war, and from him has descended a tradition of honor and glory to heroes which other epic eras do not have: the Norse, for example, wherein shrewdness was admired, intellectual power disdained (Mime), and the slaughters which occurred in great bursts of rage

were sung. Personal valor in war was a normal thing for the Norse, not worthy of any emphasis. We sons of Homer have inherited the exaltation of valor in battle, and could also recognize in it a dark destiny or a damnation. This is a true Homeric question, and all the disputes which have accrued to the historical personality of Homer are vain.

January 26, 1940

"Evolution" is a word which I do not want to hear mentioned in the field of history. The difference between nature and the realm of human activity is that in the latter nothing is inevitable and in it, "in nuce," there is every possibility. A necessary tendency exists together with its opposites, and perhaps a tiny accident is enough to develop one rather than another to the degree of "totalitarianism." If Hitler had had more success as a housepainter . . .

Index

Index

DA